Introduction

Many people may feel there have been so many books written about the Second World War, that there is definitely no need for any more. However, apart from the evacuation of children away from areas likely to be bombed, or which might be the scene of conflict in the case of invasion, it does not seem that much has been recorded about the everyday life of children during the war years. I have interviewed and recorded the memories of men and women born between 1926 and 1936. I have included myself. Our schooldays therefore coincide with that period. In addition all the writers now live in Staffordshire and Stoke-on-Trent, though many of them were born elsewhere. We have all been aware that, very soon, there will be no survivors to record their personal accounts of war time school days. Some of our writers have expressed their opinion that their memoirs would have no general interest, though some have already written accounts of what happened during those years, chiefly for the benefit of their descendants. However, I think that the record of any experiences of what it was like to live in those conditions is both educational and entertaining. I have analysed the memoirs according to their content, except for two, which are included in full. I have tried to differentiate between purely personal experiences of growing up, and the kind of experiences remembered particularly because they were related to some aspect of the war.

The first day of the War

It is interesting that all of our writers remember the first day of the war. We gathered that something very interesting, and very grave was going to happen. Probably this is because we had heard our elders and betters talking about the First World War, known to us as the Great War. Our parents were mostly middle aged in 1939, so they had had first hand experience of serving in the war, or had some direct connection with it. As you will read, the reactions of those around us to the news were in themselves memorable to us, and helped to imprint that first day on our consciousness.

Strictly speaking Peter Bruce`s war began before war was officially declared, as he was in Aberdovey, on the last day of his summer holiday with his parents.

As he recalls:
"Sept. 1st 1939 was a very hot Friday in Aberdovey. It was the next to the last day of our annual family holiday. It was also the last day of the normal peaceful world of an ordinary school boy. Germany had invaded Poland; the history of Europe was changed for ever....Aberdovey was invaded by an army of evacuees from London and the inner city areas. Hundreds of children and a handful of adults were marched from the railway station to the church hall to await allocation amongst the population of Aberdovey. I remember being told that it was lucky that our holiday was ending on Saturday as all holiday visitors were being instructed to vacate their accommodation and all hotel and boarding house keepers were given a quota of evacuated families."

Marion`s memories show that people knew and understood what evacuation would mean before the official outbreak.
"The day war broke out there was a minor skirmish going on already in our street. Our gang of kids were arguing over whose turn it was to turn the skipping rope. The neighbours shouted `The sooner you little buggers are evacuated, the sooner we`ll `ave some peace around `ere. I `ope they get yer doing something useful like potato pickin`. When the tired sad voice of Mr. Chamberlain came over the wireless later on, announcing that we were at war

with Germany, Dad`s face was grave but to me, it all seemed as though something exciting was afoot. When later on we were all told to gather in the schoolyard, with the minimum of luggage, and a luggage label with our name was threaded through a buttonhole in our coats and we were driven to the station in Liverpool, it was all so active and exciting. At Crewe we met hundreds of other children, and kindly lady helpers to check us all. One of them stitched up a hole in my haversack. Then we were dispatched on coaches to villages and hamlets. The council estate I was sent to was a hamlet of only 6 council houses, a shop and a chapel and some farms scattered around. I had to write a postcard to Mum and Dad. `Dear Mum and Dad, it is lovely here, there are fields and fields of grass –love Marion.`"

I myself was living in Essex and was playing on my own while my mother listened to the grave news. I heard Mr. Chamberlain announcing that we were at war with Germany after the chimes of Big Ben for eleven a.m. on Sunday morning, 3rd September. I rushed into the kitchen, to see Mother standing on a step ladder, putting up blackout curtains. She was crying, she didn`t realise I had seen her. I never saw her cry again.

I realised afterwards that she was crying because she had lived through the First War, and knew all the implications. Dad had been in the trenches, and she must have thought it would be the same all over again, only it would be her son this time, who would be at the sharp end. In fact he was to be in mortal danger often, as he spent 4 years of the War in the Navy, having been in a destroyer defending the ships in convoys going to Russia, and later on in the Mediterranean, both extremely dangerous and uncomfortable theatres of War, as of course were all theatres of war. I knew we were in for something dreadful, as the knowledge of what an enemy was came from my Aunt, with whom I had been to the seaside a few weeks earlier. She had been standing on the waves` edge, pointing far out into the North Sea, and had said `Our friend the Enemy.` An enquiry as to what this meant, had elicited a kind of explanation about what was going on in the big world outside our own little cosy family society.

We all knew then by the attitude of the adults that something dreadful had occurred. Many of the contributors remember the actual moment.
"I was at Junior school when war broke out. I was nine. Everyone was called

into the hall after playtime, and they told us that war had broken out, we were at war with Germany. We didn`t know what it meant; we didn`t even know where Germany was."

"My first memory of my father was standing in our living room with his back to the fireplace hearing the radio announce that we were at war with Germany. I was about four and a half years old. Both my parents were born in 1899 and my father had been conscripted in the last years of the First World War"

"I was in South London, aged 6 and heard the words `war has been declared`, and I wondered what it meant."

"I was ten years old when the war started. I was at Meir Heath and remember standing looking over the Aerodrome wondering what was going to happen."

Some writers do not recall the actual day, but do remember the occasion when they first realised what war meant.

"I was six on the first time the air raids sounded. My father was rather excitable and he opened the bedroom window and blew a whistle which had been given to him by the head air raid warden in our street. It was to be blown only if and when there was a GAS attack. Dad was in disgrace and had to give back the whistle."

"The first thing I remember about the war was going to be fitted with gas masks. I was upset because my four year old sister had a Mickey Mouse one, and I had to have a black one like the grown ups because I was six.

"I sensed an atmosphere of distraction amongst the adults (in August 1939) which I did not try to analyse. I remember Poland being invaded by the Germans. We had an elderly nanny in the house and she had a heart attack on the 3rd September and could never help out with the new baby."

"In the summer of 1939, there was open talk of the probability of war, but it was not brought home to me until the beginning of August, when a telegram arrived at our house; something of such grave importance that my father had to be told at once. I think Eddie was sent to tell him about it, and he was home within the hour. Then we were afraid. For the only time in my life I saw my mother in hysterics. My father took her into the little bedroom and the sound of wild, abandoned weeping came through the door for minutes that seemed like hours. My father had had his call up papers to join the army. He was called up so early as he had been a regular soldier, and was a member of the Territorials."

Isabel knew little about what was going on, but the nature of the reactions of neighbours which she describes were memorable.

"I was in the back yard, swinging this little girl round"

"I know where I was when War was declared on 3rd September, 1939. I was then nine and a half years old, and I was in the back-green, where a little knot of neighbours had gathered and I was swinging a little girl, round and round by the waist. My father was on what might have been his first leave. Suspense about the various peace negotiations had been growing, fuelled by radio broadcasts and news headlines and things had reached a crucial point. Someone joined us with the news. I can't remember the actual words, but I remember the gravity on people's faces and perhaps a submerged excitement. `That's that, then` somebody said. `We're at war! `"

Peter Gillard was six and a half when the Second World War `broke out`. For a six year old he was extremely alive to what was going on in the big wide world. "I can recall the pre-war anxious discussions re `Hitler`, and `Munich` and similar, between my parents, but it did not mean a lot to me, at the time, although we regularly had wounded and displaced or homeless men, some with their wives, at our front door. These were First World War victims from twenty years before, but they were still `around` all that time later. We would feed them and give them hot tea, and they would sit on the grass verge in the lane outside the house. So these people, so neglected in the `land fit for heroes`, were all I understood about `war` and its effects." Peter remembers the actual day the war started. "I can clearly recall the wireless broadcast when Chamberlain announced that `we were at war with Germany`. Then everything went quiet until the issue of `call-up` became a worry. For Father, it meant the departure of three or four men from his business, and a huge amount of extra work for him, which bore its fruit later, in 1945."

"Gas drill in the shelter"

Evacuation

Surely the most traumatic event that a child can experience is to be separated from family at an early age. There was wholesale removal of children from crowded city areas during the early weeks of the war and then again under the threat of invasion in 1940. People were ordered to register their children and then send them to collection points for removal to the country. 827,000 school children and 103,000 helpers and teachers went with them. There were also 524,000 pre-school children with their mothers who were also sent away. For some, evacuation did not last long, as the bombing of large cities did not start at the beginning of the war, so some went home after a few weeks when the air raid shelters in cities had been built. But then they had to be sent away for a second time in 1940 when London was blitzed along with many other cities, and this went on for two more years and the threat of invasion became very real. For many living in cities, evacuation to the country brought the war earlier than it began officially. This removal from home for children, as well as adults, caused much fear and distress, as will be seen reflected in these memoirs, again and again. Before the coming of television, and cheap travel, people who lived in towns had little idea of what it was like to be a country dweller, the same vice versa. The same was true about social classes. There were absolute barriers between classes, and even language barriers, between different parts of the country. Dialects were still spoken, for instance in the Forest of Dean, and in the Potteries, and even where there was no great use of different dialects, there were still strong regional accents. All this contributed to the fear shown by many host families towards having strangers arriving in their midst and by the evacuees who sometimes had difficulties in adapting.

Evacuation began before war was even declared. Plans for war were started the previous year, when Chamberlain returned from Munich after the invasion of Czechoslovakia. Experts predicted that wholesale bombing of cities would occur, as it had in Spain in the Civil War. The stories collected for this book show how many of the writers have clear memories of those first days and weeks of evacuation.

"I was born on 1st April 1926 and was evacuated with most of my school friends, a few days before war was declared. My family lived in Southampton which, being a major port, was considered a prime target for German bombs. We were put on a train, with our cardboard boxes containing gas masks, and sent off into Berkshire where various families had volunteered to take in children from more vulnerable parts of the country. My adopted family consisted of the headmaster of the local school, his sickly wife and teenage son, and I soon settled down with another girl who had also been given a temporary home. I was thirteen, and my younger brother, who was eighteen months younger than I, was sent to another village where he settled happily with a couple who had no children and he was cherished and remained in touch with them for the rest of his life.

We attended the village school every afternoon and the local children went to school in the mornings. Our teachers from our original school taught us so there was continuity of teaching, although rather less than normal. My fellow evacuee was two years younger than me, and developed the habit of wetting the double bed that we shared and apparently this was a common problem with displaced children, who had outgrown the habit, but no-one seemed to realise the stress which affected them.

Our hostess was not at all well, and the strain began to show on her, so it was decided that we should be moved from that address. I was sent to the local manor house, and was lodged with the maids and was the only child in the house. I did not last long as I made the mistake of getting a tray for the girl I shared a bedroom with when she was not feeling well. I was in the kitchen with the cook who was getting some food, when the mistress of the house appeared and I put the tray under the wooden kitchen table where everyone could see it. On being questioned I was told that no food was to be taken to bedrooms and a few days later, I was moved to a farmhouse.

I think the family were Quakers and there were two maiden ladies and a brother. They were very kind and welcoming, but I didn`t understand why we all sat in silence in church until someone was moved by the spirit to pray. The house was very old and the lavatory was at the end of the garden, so I was terrified to go out there after dark.

I was a novelty to the village boys, and they gave me presents but I was a bit bewildered by one offering which had a note attached asking if I liked "cock-a-lick" and I decided they didn`t know how to spell.

My mother used to visit me and my brother. I always begged to go home with her, although my brother was quite contented with the motherly lady who looked after him. In about six months I found myself back in Southampton." Averil.

Marion describes the excitement of leaving Liverpool.

"The weather was glorious that September of 1939 and being billeted with two other girls of my age in a three bedroomed house with a garden seemed as if it might be fun. The trouble was one of the two girls wet the bed, and that took the fun out of everything. The woman we billeted with made such a fuss, and dowsed all our spirits. She succeeded in making us all feel guilty, besides the poor little girl herself who cried and sobbed. The billeting officer was called in and she got an earful too. The mattress was shown to the neighbours, and the whole hamlet was aware of our hostess` martyrdom. There should have been rubber sheets available, I suppose, but everything was in an upheaval as the bombing was expected any time on Liverpool Docks. In the

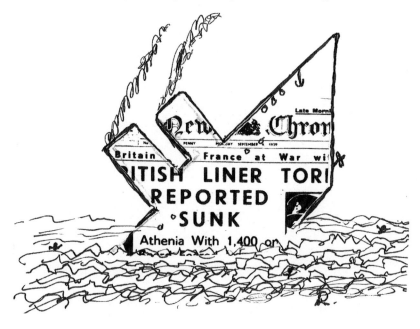

event that did not happen for two years. There was no school to attend as there were too many evacuees for the small village school to cope with. So we had the run of the fields and the farm. The lanes were traffic-free and we played in the hedges and ditches, explored the small wood on the knoll, picked the ripening corn, and made strings of beads with it, played hide and seek, and made ourselves useful in the house. It was a happy time; and save for the bed-wetting incident, only one other bit of bother occurred for the 6 weeks I was there. In the big house on the corner, one evacuee made a lot of trouble by writing home and telling terrible tales of how wicked the woman was who was looking after her. The billeting office came again and then the woman's daughter arrived as well. The two local women both started crying, so there they were, the two of them, in the lane with a crowd around them, sobbing into their pinnies at the terrible lies which had been written about them. A small crowd of sympathisers stood round, witnessing their martyrdom, (the second in the village in a month.) To have a peaceful Sunday afternoon several of us evacuees were sent to Sunday school, along with some of the more pious of the village children. It was held in a small chapel by a horrid narrow-minded woman with a silly hat on and a more boring afternoon, I considered, would be hard to find. Half way through the afternoon, the woman realised I was not wearing a hat, and humiliated me by being scandalized by it, and making me wear a rain hood she fished out of her pocket. I felt such a `Charlie` sitting there, reading the bible and wearing a rain hood, when it wasn't even raining and it was indoors anyway, and the roof wasn't leaking. I refused to go again. I remember the thrill of delight when I heard the sound of Dad`s voice in the hall. He had bought a house in a village outside Liverpool, and had come to get me home".

It was not unusual for children to be evacuated when the war began, and then for them to be returned home, as no bombing raids had taken place. Then a few short weeks after, the war would begin in earnest, and they would be right in the thick of it.

At least two of our writers had narrow escapes from what would have been a fatal evacuation. My father and mother determined that we would escape the horrors of war by being brought up by Canadian relatives. Dad`s plan was to emigrate to Canada after the war anyway. So we were all booked up to go there in the various evacuation schemes being organised at the outbreak of war. However, after a few weeks, my parents changed their minds. (One liner carrying children was sunk on the day after war began.)

Another writer recalls "I almost got evacuated to the USA to my father's brother, still have all the documents, and was all ready to pack and go, but didn`t because of the sinking of a liner with evacuees on, many lost their lives."

"She humiliated me
by making me wear
a rain-hood"

Rules and Regulations.

Because of the outbreak of War, Britain virtually became a police state. We just knew that we had to do what we were told. Helen says it all.

"The outbreak of war brought many rules, regulations, shortages, deprivations and the chronological details of each escape me. However, I remember gas masks were early on the agenda – Each child and adult was fitted with the masks in the village school, shown how to use it and fit it into the box, and how to wear it across the shoulder when leaving the house. No one knew the nature of the impending warfare. Identity cards, ration books, clothing coupons all followed together with strict "blackout" instructions for houses. There was a type of tape put on the inside of window frames which proved very effective when the sirens sounded. `Moaning Minnie` and `Wailing Winnie`" were almost as much a focus in the village as the church, situated side-by side on the hilltop.

Blast from a high explosive bomb might well have shattered the glass one side of our house the following year."

We children in those days were quite used to being strictly disciplined, and so a few more regulations made little difference. We soon got used to being obliged to carry round gas-masks, and having to adhere to blackout regulations, and rationing.

Rules of all kinds were stricter and more numerous, because of it being wartime. We shall see how the blackout and rationing affected people's lives. As there were so many service personnel wandering about in strange places, far from home, it might have been expected that adults would be more worried about the safety of their children, however none of the writers felt there was any threat from the young men. (This was at the start of the war. It became different on the arrival of American troops.) In the beginning, people felt having soldiers nearby was more of a protection than a threat. This was a contrast to the attitude taken by my boarding school, later on. Alerted by the presence of so many American troops in the town girls were forbidden to walk down the High Street. The strict rules about where we could go were understandable, as if anything had happened to one of us, the school would soon have gone out of business.

Travel

Before the War most civilians did little travelling. Although by 1939, middle aged men may have had to travel to the various theatres of war in the previous conflict when they were youths, many town dwellers had only been to nearby seaside resorts, or perhaps to visit relatives, in the country, for day trips or for the annual holiday. Travel was looked upon as an adventure. It turned out to be a very nasty experience for the duration of the war. Some extracts from our writers show this.

"Saturday, 2nd September, 1939, we leave for home. We leave Aberdovey early in the morning, we change trains at Machynlleth, Chester and Crewe. When we arrive at Crewe it is already getting dark …there are no lights on the station except for an occasional dimly lit portable oil lamp…blackout already implemented. When the Stoke train finally arrives it is quite dark, the windows of the carriage have been painted dark blue, as well as the electric light. Notices tell passengers not to open windows during hours of darkness, or to display any light. At each station en route the porter shouts its name, without this it is impossible to know where we are. When we arrive home we struggle in the dark to search for temporary material to black out the windows before we can turn the lights on.

On Sunday September 3rd 1939 we go off to Sunday School but return in time to listen to the Prime Minister's announcement at 11 am that we are now officially at war with Germany. Later in the war we were able to journey for days out and short holidays, as some travel restrictions were lifted. We went to Blackpool and were thrilled to see the town practically taken over by the RAF all being drilled and in various duties. There were huge fortifications below the tide line, to stop any invasion, and low flying exercises too. The journey from Stoke to Blackpool took between three and a half to five hours, and we had dubious meat pies and hard rock cakes in the station buffets, with weak tea. The trains often had no corridor, and were filthy, and crowded with service personnel on the move.

Because of petrol rationing, the number of cars on the road was minimal.

"Everyone took to their bikes. The roundsmen for groceries, coal, milk, bread and general haulage contractors used horse drawn vehicles. In our family of five, all except Mother were cyclists. We visited beauty spots, did the shopping, and enjoyed, as never before or since, the traffic free roads."

(I had such traffic free experience when our local main road was closed for re-building a road bridge, after a big flood in the 1970`s. It was bliss for walkers and cyclists.)

Peter Gillard. explains some of the difficulties facing those who ran public buses in rural Devon. "Buses were run on coal gas, in some cases, generated by a coke furnace towed behind the bus. The gas was piped to the adapted engine. On steep hills (common in North Devon) all able bodied adults and children would have to get off the bus at the bottom of the hill (for example, Dean Steep) on the Lynmouth to Barnstaple road, so that the bus could make its asthmatic climb up the hill! The fumes from the gas would cause passengers to suffer bad headaches; in fact the onset of possible carbon monoxide poisoning. My young brother Colin, was so affected In this way on one occasion that he had to be taken off the bus part way up the hill."

My best school friend lived only 14 miles from us. That seemed a long way. I would sometimes bike over there, in the holidays, and on one occasion I was overtaken by one vehicle only. I myself overtook a farm cart. I returned with the bike on the train. Sometimes my friend and I would meet half way, by going on the train. These local trains were all right, but travelling on the main lines was awful, crowded and dirty, with hardly any non-smoking carriages, so one was suffocated with tobacco smoke, and foul loos, blocked and filthy. It was almost better to sit in the corridor, on a suitcase, the air was slightly clearer but there was the hazard of being kicked and buffeted by other passengers, going back and forth to the lavatories and all the horrors of disgusting smells. Besides all the discomforts, and the trains being dreadfully delayed, there were some nice people on trains, who would share food with us children.

Bicycle and train, bus and "Shanks pony" were our main means of transport because of the petrol shortage. This made life very stressful for emergency workers and including doctors. As Brenda says:-
"My father had some nightmare journeys trying to find his way up the hills in Leek to deliver babies. You had half a headlight, the rest blacked out and there were no signposts in case the Germans landed."

At school we walked from our houses down to lessons. No bicycles were allowed for younger pupils. In fact we walked long distances to get to games and church, too.

The ownership of a motor car was not a possibility for most working people, but for those who did enjoy this privilege, pre-war, this soon came to an end. In the first place, petrol was strictly rationed, to those who really needed it for their jobs, e.g. medical doctors, and executive and administrative personnel. Otherwise, people had to use public transport. Peter Gillard recalls; "Mr Lile had a car, which like many others had to be `laid up for the duration of the war' which was supposed to be potentially brief! Eventually, as with others, the car was requisitioned for reasons of National Defence, leaving the garage usable for other purposes."

Shelters

Some of the most vivid recollections of our writers were about their time spent down in the air raid shelters. As Peter Bruce recalls:

"Every class had to make its way in a quick but orderly fashion down to the allocated shelter. All our shelters were underground, constructed by building a trench about ten foot deep and then bricking the sides and putting on a 12 inch concrete roof. Several feet of earth were then thrown on the roof. These shelters were supposed to be safe against any bombing except a direct hit by a very large high explosive bomb. Each shelter held about a hundred people and it was extremely damp and cold. Although several day time raids did take place no actual enemy attacks occurred, and the raids were of short duration. Most of the children rather enjoyed this diversion from normal school work for while we were in the shelter the teachers organised community singing. "Run Rabbit Run," and "Roll out the Barrel" were top of the pops at that

Anderson shelter in the garden.

time, along with "We're going to hang out our washing on the Siegfried line" though after the collapse of France we sang that no more." (The Siegfried Line was a heavily fortified line built by the Germans to protect their borders).

Other writers give us a clear picture what sheltering was about.
"An Anderson shelter was delivered to every householder who wanted one

and had space for it. When ours arrived Dad and his brother dug a four foot hole in the garden in order to partially submerge the corrugated iron shelter, and then piled earth on top. This was to be our refuge during the bombing raids that occurred nightly during the winter of 1940/1"

"We had an air raid shelter in the back yard and there was a bigger one in Oak St, around the corner, a brick one, but it always smelt of pee, the men came out of the pub and peed in it. The sirens would go off and we would go off to school with our gas masks on."

"Our shelter was the coal cellar; later on we had a shelter in the garden with beds. Don't remember being in it very much. We all slept downstairs. Brown paper strips criss-crossed over windows to stop, as far as possible, glass shattering into room. Woke up alone in the shelter one morning in a strange dawn light and thought I was the only survivor. Luckily not so."

"Later on this shelter was fitted up with bunk beds, a floor and bit of carpet and a box with batteries and bulbs and a hole through the lid to give us some light, with the door safely closed of course, the condensation ran down the walls, but we survived it all. I found a four leaved clover growing in the soil covering it, and took it as a good luck sign."

"We went to school half days alternately with other classes whilst the school shelters were being built. They seemed a long way to run to when we had practice. Thankfully we never had an air raid. "

Shelter life was a great leveller, as all of a household, even the fairly wealthy employers, would share the same shelter, and the same fear, as the servants.

"At the beginning of the war we would all sit under the stairs when there was an air raid, then like everyone else we built a shelter, ours was in the garden, and always smelt of earth. We scrambled down a ladder to get to it. The maids used to come down in their curlers, our father was usually up at the hospital and our mother stayed at the top watching the fires where the Germans had dropped bombs on Crewe, an important railway junction.

Many writers have commented on the way people kept their spirits up when in the shelters.

"When the sirens blew to announce enemy planes were overhead, we all went into the brick shelter in a corner of the school yard. There we sat in the semi-dark, with a retired teacher who had come back to help out, and she sang nursery rhymes and told stories, until the `All Clear` sounded. The warning was an imperative whoop, whoop, whoop; the all clear was a long, steady, wail."

Even houses in the depths of the country were advised to make shelters as Peter Gillard recollects.

"The flimsy garage (vacated by the requisitioned car....see above) was transformed into a shelter for we fifteen or so little children. I am sure we would have been safer in the house or under the massive garden hedge! BUT the issue was not only shelter, but safety from the greater menace of a `gas attack`. Thus the door to the garage was surrounded by a framework, from which hung two old blankets. Water in two watering cans was stored close by. In the event of the sirens going off, we would scurry to the shelter and await the police or ARP warning of an imminent gas attack. At this Mrs.Lile would wet the blankets with the water to keep out the gas!

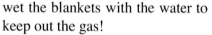

All this was inspected and approved by the relevant authorities. Serious stuff! We never got bombed, let alone gassed."

Strangely enough, we had no shelter, although our house was right next door to the perimeter fence of a massive explosives factory. My father had to occupy this as he was the Superintendent of the factory which was situated in among the dunes and marshes of the South Wales Coast, not far from Swansea. Quite a dangerous place, I should have thought, well meriting a shelter. Mother turned down the offer of a Morrison shelter, a kind of hugely strong table with wire guard, to put in the living room.

Helen says:-

"Our cellar consisted of two large and one smaller room. A trap door in the small room led to an L shaped room which we called the "bogey hole" a special den where William smoked his first cigarettes and we had "gang" meetings with our friends.

In the cellar's largest room there was a double bed for parents, a large pram for Dorothy, a bunk bed for William and me and a single for Norah and Jean. There was another single bed in the small room easily accessible to the cellar steps for anyone on call for either the hospital or fire–fighting duty or for a visitor trapped in our house over-night by a raid.

I remember the siren "Moaning Minnie" not with fear so much as excitement in the daytime. At school it meant leaving the classroom and going to underground Big Hall till Wailing Winnie sounded safety."

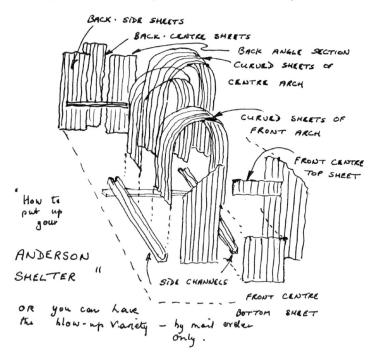

Gas masks and the blackout

I have given a separate section to those grim pieces of equipment as they were such a potent signal that we were all under attack, no matter where or when. The general opinion was that the gas attacks on soldiers in trenches during the 1914-18 war was the most barbaric method of killing or maiming people ever invented, and there seemed little protection to be had against this cowardly and inhuman behaviour of the enemy in employing this tool. We all therefore obediently carried our gas masks everywhere, during the first few months after the outbreak of war. The gas attacks never came, and we consigned the gas masks to the cupboards under the stairs. Also, the little cardboard box, slung over the shoulder, was a sign that we children were taking things seriously, and if we didn`t have this accoutrement, the local `little Hitlers (in our estimation) viz the Air Raid Wardens and the local bobbies, took the chance to assert their authority in no uncertain terms. Peter Bruce recounts that

"during the first year or two of the war all children had to take their gas masks to school and carry them with them wherever they went and gas mask drill was an everyday exercise.

For a while, I deliberately forgot to bring the mask to school, and was promptly sent home again. Being a lazy boy who enjoyed play far more than school, for a short while I thought I had found a panacea for enforced education. It wasn't long however before my teacher decided that my gas mask amnesia could be permanently cured by a single application of the cane."

Although there were never any gas air raids, the first few months of the war were dominated by the fear of them. Thus children remember the practices for a gas raid.

"We also had to practise wearing our gas masks during lessons, they smelt horrible and were very hot."

The other instant and burdensome sign of the war, was the infamous `blackout`, when the lights did literally go out. Streets were totally unlit after a certain hour, in urban areas. I don't remember much of this, as our house was in a rural situation, where we were used to finding our way down lanes by star or moonlight.

Isabel's memory of the blackout is that every effort was made by the authorities to
"get this right in the beginning with a surplus of zeal that, nevertheless, paid off. Broadcasts were made emphasising the importance of keeping our positions secret from enemy bombers in the night and instructions were given on what kind of blinds to use to achieve a complete absence of light. The ARP (Air Raid Precaution Unit) were put in charge of enforcing this and could make you conform by plastering up any little pin-point or edge of light that you had missed. Torches were allowed, but again the aim was for minimum light, so some people conscientiously cut out circles of black paper with a hole in the middle and placed them behind the glass, where they cut down the beam to a feeble glow. Inevitably you would sometimes be caught in the dark without a torch. Like most families, we had taken the bulb out of the light in our lobby to avoid its spilling out the light into the stair well, and I was groping my way towards the front door, with my hands held before me, when I walked straight into it edge-on with my nose, feeling vainly on either side of the already open door. My brother Eddie fell ill and this made progress to and from the shelter during air-raids impossible without Mr. Anthony, our friendly ARP man. He was not very tall or robust, but he must have had sinews like steel. He made my mother promise to stay put until he got there, (which was always within minutes of the start of a raid), got Eddie, a tall, gangly, thirteen year old, onto his shoulder, in a fireman's lift and got him to the shelter, doing the journey again at the end of a raid. Sometimes we would offer him a cup of tea in the middle of the night before he went home."

The task of putting up the blackout was swiftly and conscientiously carried out. Marion describes the stress of having to do it, and then keep it up all through the war until the bombing was over, except for the unmanned plane and rocket attacks which took place after Allied troops finally landed in France in 1944. Some of the regulations seem unbelievable petty with hindsight.

"Putting up blackout curtains was a right pain as only tacks were available to keep the black out curtain material close enough to the window to stop the light showing outside. Double, thick curtains were really needed. One way of keeping the light from shining was by painting the top of the shades black, and keeping the lights low and focussed on the objects, in other words, no top lights in the ceiling. Any chinks showing brought the dreaded `knock` on the door by the warden or policemen who spied it. Flash lamps were also hooded and if you went out in the dark, you had to walk carefully, as street lighting was non existent, and the flash lamp had to be pointed down. I remember going out with the pram and we had a lamp fixed at the front of it so no one would bump into it."

Go by SHANKS' PONY and leave room for those who have longer journeys.

Changes in the Environment, and in Living Conditions.

The war started slowly. Peter Bruce describes what happened as the months went on. "The summer of 1940 was one of glorious summer weather. The fall of France in June ended the period known as the phoney war when except for the blackout, life on the surface in North Staffordshire was relatively uneventful The fear of imminent invasion changed the concept of war overnight. The area became a beehive of activity. All signposts were removed in order to confuse the enemy in the event of invasion, iron railings and gates were removed from schools and other buildings (as well as houses), to provide iron and steel for war production (they were never used), and large static water tanks, (for the fire engines, and maybe even for household use if the water supply were to be cut off) were built at intervals in all built up areas."

Helen's memories are similar:
"There were physical changes to our local environment: street lights were not lit, iron railings were removed, sandbags were in abundance to protect low windows and strict blackout regulations were adhered to or fines were imposed".

All through the war, as Helen recalls, even the copious water supplies which anyone living in Britain always takes for granted, were in short supply.
"Living conditions were Spartan, with 5 inches of water in the twice weekly bath, a low temperature of the heating system, and only such clothing as the coupon allowance permitted – very little mufti –although there were people clever with the needle and thread. That meant people were cold and had chilblains."

There was "Plenty of rain, but shortage of water. Severe winters, but shortage of coal."

As the war went on, more remote areas began to feel its impact as well. Whereas it was the South East area which witnessed the Battle of Britain going on in the skies above, by the summer of 1944 it was the South West, which saw the build up of troops being assembled for the D Day landings in Normandy.

In Peter Gillard's words,
"Nearer D Day, which was on 6th June, 1944, there were huge fleets of landing craft along the estuary and coast, ready for the Allies to land in Europe and start the liberation of countries occupied by the Germans under Nazi rule. They suddenly disappeared as the second wave of invading troops got underway. A USA `Liberty Ship` was torpedoed off the coast and made it into the estuary at high tide and was secured to the tide`s edge near Instow. It seemed huge – about 6000 tons- I think it remained there until long after the war was over.
The bracketed pavements on the Long Bridge were menaced with collapse as a result of the passage of American tanks over the mediaeval structure and only one tank was allowed to pass over at a time."

'Warm by the fire while doing our mending.

Displacement

As mentioned above, people had to get used to having to move about the country, whether to get away from the bombing, or because families tried to live closer to fathers who had been sent to different areas because of their work and war service

Isabel recalls her new life:
"Our junior school, in common with most others, temporarily closed down and our whole family moved to be near my father's posting at Gifford, a small beautiful village about twenty miles south-east of Edinburgh. We were billeted near the army camp, so we were well placed to enter these two very different worlds at will.
We used to visit the camp every day and were possibly the only challenge to the soldiers at that time. We were drilled to check our headlong rush across the fields at the words, "Halt, who goes there?"
"A friend," we would answer, whether we were one, two three or four.
"One friend," came the answer." Step forward and be recognised!" the sentry would say.
We would then take a single step forward and collapse, giggling. Sometimes we wouldn't see my father, but got a report as to where he was, and reassured, we would return to the other world…playing in the woods….picking hazel nuts…. balancing across the tumbling burn…it was our first undiluted taste of rural life, all the sweeter for being stolen from the harsher reality of school. This idyllic life soon came to an end, and since there had been no bombing so far, lessons were offered for half days, in church halls. The schools were being used for distribution of gas masks and ration books. The church halls were unheated and we were allowed to keep our coats and even gloves on, as the weather got colder. My mother made my younger sister wear fawn knitted pantaloons, with an elastic under the instep. We did homework with friends, in the afternoon, which my mother supervised."

Georgina's family had to move also.
"Fortunately for us my father was seconded to the Ministry of Food and we went to North Wales. No raids. Realised we were a bit deaf, but recovered.

American soldiers in the area, convoys of tanks going through, and caterpillar tracks making shattering noise on the road."

In some cases the whole school moved, as Brenda states. The change of location was sometimes unpleasant, sometimes not so bad.
"Because of the bombs Virginia and I were sent to the Edgbaston Church of England School which had been evacuated to Attingham Park in Shropshire. Lord Berwick still lived there. We were in the basement, we were utterly miserable. It was cold and damp, and we lived on rabbit. I remember perpetual earache. It was set in lovely grounds, parkland, and there were lots of red squirrels. We lasted one term.
Next we went to Malvern, plus our nanny, to stay with our Aunt and Uncle and two cousins. It must have been dreadful for them because our nanny made us sit at meals until we had finished every bit. We were always told to remember the starving children in Europe. I hated it when our cousins called us refugees. There were nice times, they had two fat rabbits and we used to feed them dandelions."

"The Americans gave us cigarettes we could swap."

Rhona recalls her move.
"During the war we spent 4 years in Wendover, Bucks, (near Aylesbury) and

then in Ely, Cambridgeshire. The 4 years in one place was because my father was abroad in the war, most of that time (3 years). Altogether my sister and I went to seven or eight schools. The education I received at one of these, a convent, was excellent and the regime strict. We walked thirty minutes' over wild heathland to get there. The second school was enjoyable and less strict, and we travelled by train to Aylesbury after a fifteen minutes walk to the station. The journeys to both schools were unaccompanied, (unheard of these days for 8 - 12 year olds.) The reason why we had to move so often was because my father was in the R.A.F. This resulted in our not making friends at school as we never stayed long enough to make good friends."

I myself left the school which we had formerly travelled to by car, and attended one in a nearby town, which we went to on our bikes. My companion was a small boy, aged 7. I was 9. We made the cycle journey for two terms, going 4 miles there and 4 miles back, on our own, and thought nothing of it. When families had enough money, the children were sometimes sent away to boarding schools.

Helen describes how she felt.
"Before elaborating on life based at home in the first half of the war, a parental decision was made that in Sept 1939 I would become a weekly boarder at St Dominic's Catholic School. Thus I left home for the first time. I was eight. Presumably this was an attempt by my parents to lessen the pressures of adaptation to wartime living and to help my mother cope, as she was late in pregnancy. William had moved to St Josephs, Trent Vale as a day boy and Jean was a toddler of 2. Both stayed at home. The boarding experience was not a happy one, and it made a deep impression on me and in a way, one could say that this experience was due to the war. The nuns were very kind, but the huge dormitory, with high arched ceiling and no light except for a few candles, was scary, with most of the girls being older and not known to me. I spent a lot of free time in the church attending Mass and Benediction each day and purchased holy pictures and a rosary. I had heard that William and I might be sent to Seattle, Washington U.S.A. on a convoy with other children, to stay with relations for the duration of the war. (Our maternal grandmother was American, although she lived in England from 1901 onwards) This possibility worried me intensely and I prayed at the various statues to this numinous God who was directing my fate."

My own father was an industrial chemist. He had served for part of the 1914 war, in the trenches, and had then been brought back to work as a chemist in the ordnance factory which was producing explosives, at Litherland, near Liverpool. So his knowledge and experience were very valuable. He offered his services to the War Department in 1939 and was immediately sent to South Wales, to work in the Royal Ordnance Factory at Pembrey, working, once again, on explosives. Mother and he decided that they must find accommodation near his work, and in the summer of 1940 Dad finally managed to rent a house for us near to his work, in South Wales. I remember our going on the train from our house in the countryside in Essex. As we boarded the train, I climbed in with my cricket bat, with a book tied on to it. My sister complained that I looked like a refugee, with my possessions tied up with string. Mother said `We are refugees, aren't we?` In later years, when we returned home, we were teased that we had `run away` in 1940. Well, many people did run away, if that is the right word, when you go to avoid bombing or invasion. In any case, it seemed to me that we were even more in the eye of danger, by living right next door to an explosives factory. We children did not worry about the wrongs or rights, we just went with the family, and our displacement to South Wales has always seemed to me to be the happiest time of my childhood. My father was with us all the time, as had not been the case formerly, owing to his business commitments away from home, in the previous period of my childhood. Also, my mother went off to work in the factory, and although we children felt lonely during the day, we had unlimited amounts of freedom, together with responsibility for ourselves, a marvellous way to grow up. Displacement has always seemed to me to be a formative experience, as long as your loved ones are still nearby.

Later, in 1941, I was sent to Cheltenham, to board at a prestigious school . This was yet another displacement, and not such a happy experience.

Helen, from Stoke-on-Trent, has written about her memory of being sent away from home for the second time, during the war. Helen and I met years later, in the course of writing this book.

She says; "In 1942 I was sent to Cheltenham to be a boarder again. I had reached the end of Upper 2 at St. Dominic's, and I thought it was up into the Senior School with my friends…but no, I was to be a boarder and out into the unknown; though in truth my mother did take me to look at it, on the train from Stoke. I was duly impressed by the look of it, but I didn't get the feel of it until going in September.

There were other changes at this time; my two young sisters were evacuated to Wales with another family, in the care of two nannies in a Guest House in Snowdonia. This left our parents to carry on their work and feel the children were safe from the bombing, I presume. As for being at boarding school, there was too much to get used to and find out about the logistics of living in a large house of over 60 girls, to feel homesick. I was in fear and trembling about what to do and where to go. …any food which we had brought from home was confiscated, ration books were handed in…all our books we had brought were checked"

As I said, the war brought some freedom of behaviour to some children, who had been brought up to strict codes of behaviour, until the disruptions of moving and the absence of one or both parents loosened some of the restrictions which they had formerly experienced. In our family, as my mother was working, my elder sister, in her school holidays, ruled the roost, and her rule was not so strict as my mother's. My other sister, and I, grew up quickly, and enjoyed our freedom. When we went off to boarding school, it was suddenly different. We weren't to put our hands in our pockets, we had to wear school hats and gloves, we weren't allowed, ever, to eat so much as a Mars bar outside, (if we could get one); the list went on of do`s and don`ts. Somehow for every new rule the Government imposed, or every restriction that propaganda suggested, there was a second one imposed by school. For instance, it was suggested by government, to save water, we should only have 5 inches of water in the bath. But our school ruled that we should only have two baths a week. There were American and Canadian soldiers stationed in Cheltenham. Because of this, not only were we banned from visiting the High Street, so that we wouldn't fall into the clutches of these soldiers, we weren't even allowed to go for walks except in carefully monitored groups of at least four. No wonder some of us grew up in fear of strangers, especially male, and some of us grew up as rebels, with a distrust of any authority. All this, was because of displacement to a totally alien environment, a side effect of the war.

Bombing and Invasion Threat.

Almost all of the writers had some experience of bombing raids. Obviously with city children this forms the overriding memory of the war. Peter Bruce, brought up in Stoke-on- Trent, writes descriptively about the raids.

"For the rest of the winter we remained huddled under the stairs at night when there were raids on. It was very frightening particularly when the bombs were dropped locally. The long loud whistle of the bomb which sometimes lasted for as long as ten to fifteen seconds followed by a tremendous explosion that shook the very earth around you, was a terrifying experience."

My own experience of bombing was slight; nevertheless it made a lasting impression.

I had first hand knowledge of only two bombs being dropped in the nearby vicinity, during the war. Considering that our home was right outside the perimeter fence of an explosives factory in South Wales, for the last four years of the war, this is quite amazing. The first bomb I heard dropping was one which came down on Barnstaple where I lived with my sister, during the autumn of 1940. We had just gone to bed, and I was lying awake. I heard the chimes of Big Ben from the radio downstairs, and just as the last chime went, there was a huge screaming whistle, and then a massive bang, which shook the house. We both leapt out of bed, raced down the stairs, and hid under the stairs with our Aunt. Uncle went outside to see if he could see anything. For the rest of the War, I dreaded the nine-o-clock chimes, thinking that they might mean there were bombs ready to drop, up there. I could distinguish the drone which bombers made, as opposed to the noise our fighters made. Usually it was just one plane up there, some airman must have lost his way, and the bomb that landed near us was being discarded by the German pilot who was trying to get home. At school in Cheltenham, later on, we had one massive high explosive bomb in the same street. I don't remember hearing it, but remember peering at the huge crater where the once proud Victorian house had stood in its own grounds of cedar trees and laurels.

The other terrifying experience of a bombing raid was when my sisters and I were making our way back from South Wales to Cheltenham for the autumn term in 1941 or 1942. We had had a lovely picnic that day, with my parents on the beach at Ferryside, a short train ride from our home. We were already late, as Dad had insisted on our missing the train we were supposed to catch, and going on the last one….much to Mother's disapproval. We had no sooner got on the train, than it began to behave erratically, a fault of trains in the war. When it was already dark the train came to a halt, with no explanation from anyone. We had very dim lights in the carriage, and after muffling what little light there was, we peeped round the blackout blinds. We must have been on a mountain branch line, presumably to avoid the coast, and there, far below us, we saw a large city…it was Swansea, and all along what we took to be the sea, was a red glow…the docks burning. We couldn't hear much, but the sight of the massive fires gave a glow to the skyline, like a sunset in the middle of the night. We hastily put back the blinds, and cuddled up to each other, to comfort ourselves. Someone in the carriage offered us a little cake each, a very kind gesture in the days of rationing…people were always kind to strangers, especially to children. We eventually went on our way, skirting round Cardiff. When we finally arrived at the school, the teachers weren't cross with us for being late. They were so relieved to see us, having heard about the bombing, they took us back to the boarding house, and feasted us on cocoa, and crumpets toasted on the gas fire…such luxury at that point in the war.

Georgina lived in South London, and for her, the bombing experience was terrifying.
"Flashes in the sky, parents rushing to take me indoors, a raid on Croydon Aerodrome.
Terrific noise, lots of shrapnel falling as there was a gun emplacement and searchlight in a field at bottom of our garden, target for bombers. Once a neighbour found a machine gun bullet embedded in the floor of her landing. Gas main in road on fire, mother rushed out with stirrup pump, hopeless task. One night very near miss, bomb very close, huge noise, and broken glass came in across our beds. We were all heaped up by then, parents on top of me. …the sound of the siren….the feeling of dread induced by this sound remains till this day.
There was a big fire on the City and East End. Huge fires as publishers` warehouses burned. For several days afterwards burnt paper floated down on us. Visited London briefly when doodlebugs (unmanned bombers) were

coming over. You hear the engine, then it cuts out, and there is a pause before the bang. Where will it land?"

Helen knew what it was like to be bombed as her home was in Stoke-on-Trent. "Although the Potteries were not a prime target for German bombers, Coventry, Liverpool and Manchester suffered on a much larger scale. There was no hiding Shelton Bar Iron and Steel Works, and there were several direct hits within a mile of us. In fact it was a kind of status symbol if you turned up at school with a piece of shrapnel collected from your lawn as a result of the previous night's bombing. There were quite a few bombs around there. The bombing that really affected us was the demolition of the new nurses` home at the beginning of the war. The eye dept outpatients was destroyed the some night. Again there were no fatalities. We could see the nurses' home from our bathroom window.

Nearer to home was an incendiary bomb on the Army barracks opposite to our house. I believe only one soldier was killed. A short distance away in Newcastle Lane a semi–detached house received a direct hit and the church warden Mr Steele was killed and his wife, paralysed for three months in Oswestry Hospital, sadly died too. We were fortunate when a large high explosive bomb landed over our garden hedge in an allotment next door. It was so close and the blast mainly went upwards and over the house. The lawn and our neighbour's the other side were scattered with shrapnel; yet not one window broke on the bomb side of the house, only the pipes from the bathroom and toilet. We had not heard Minnie that night and mother was in the bathroom."

Brenda recalls the same events.
"Another series of bombs fell on the new nurses` home at the Infirmary; it had been opened on the Saturday by the Duke of Gloucester. The nurses were going to move in on the Monday and it was bombed to bits, empty by the grace of God on the Sunday. I still have the illegal film which my father took with his cine camera under his coat."

Peter Gillard, who grew up to be a skilled musician, remembers the sound of the planes.
"Occasionally the sirens would go off and we would hear the pulsing sound of the unsynchronised German engines, high over head on their way to bomb South Wales. There were one or two attempts to bomb the Coastal Command airfield at Chivenor, but without much success. One high explosive bomb fell a mile or two away, left an impressive hole and killed a donkey! The bombing of Plymouth and Exeter was on a large scale and like other cities there was much suffering and destruction. We could see the glow over Plymouth in spite of the city being 80 miles away."

Isabel also describes the noise as well as the fall-out.
"Although Edinburgh largely escaped the bombing, which reduced to rubble vast areas of Clydeside and Coventry, …raids were frequent and barrages of gunfire meant shrapnel was a credible source of danger. We came to regard the throb of enemy bombers, usually at night, as something to fear. During air raids my grandfather, if he was staying with us, always refused to budge from his bed and we would hear missiles whistling overhead and loose fragments of metal landing on rooftops from our dug-out and wonder what the outcome would be. I suppose that, having escaped death by war once, he believed himself fireproof…an old man would talk to grandpa, having been in the same regiment as him, and they would chat about old times. The scale of destruction had increased by light years from hand-to-hand engagements with either Zulus or Boers. Perhaps they felt they inhabited a different world.
Our neighbour had to go indoors one night, and her husband called out to her, "Put something on your head!" A tin tray or something protective was

34

what he had in mind, and we were all amused when she got back wearing a chiffon scarf!

My favourite shelter memory is of two little sisters, who lived at the other end of the block. They raided our shelter, and discovered the bottle of brandy and biscuits which Mother kept there for emergencies. The prank came to light when they were found reeling about the green, drunk and very, very happy.

Only two bombs fell in Edinburgh. The daytime one knocked me off my feet and under the table. We all landed in different parts of the room, but nobody was hurt. The other fell on Corstorphine Zoo, giving rise to lurid stories of dangerous animals thereby released and prowling the streets. There may have been a grain of truth in it, however. On one of his leaves before being posted abroad, my father took us to the zoo. Sometimes he arrived home with a box of sweets. They had become very scarce and we were impressed to be given a whole Mars bar each as part of the treat. For some reason, perhaps a sense of occasion, we all unwrapped them as we entered the gates and were amazed to be suddenly surrounded by clouds of birds, many brilliantly coloured budgerigars amongst them, who quite clearly wanted the Mars bars. Half horrified and half charmed, we held them up in the air, and within a minute, they had disappeared. Not a crumb was left.

Raids upset your general sleeping pattern and it happened at least once, when my friend, Molly Munro, was with us, that we talked until dawn. Then one went to the nearby baker`s for hot rolls, while the other made a pot of tea. We wasted most of the week's butter ration on the rolls – delicious."

No-one completely escaped, and to all, it was a shattering experience, as Rhona's words show.

"We were lucky in the fact that, as the German bombers flew over us to the Midlands, only one bomb dropped on the Heath, about 70 yards behind our house. We hid under the stairs at night for eighteen months."

It was not unusual for children to have been evacuated away from big cities, at the outbreak of war, to avoid any likely bombing and then, when no bombing took place during the so-called phoney war, to be allowed to go home again. Then, a few short months later, the war began in earnest, and the children were then right in the thick of it, with the big cities being bombed regularly.

"The air-raids began soon after we returned to Southampton (from being evacuated), but we had a cellar and made up beds down here and we were reasonably comfortable. My half-brother (my mother was widowed in the Great War) was eight years older than me and was serving in the R.A.F., where he spent the time in N. Africa as one of the "wingless warriors" as the Aussies dubbed them. One night, when I was fourteen, I had arranged to meet a friend at the cinema, and was walking along the road when the sirens sounded. I was ignoring them, as I was looking forward to a pleasant evening, but an elderly man came out of a public shelter (made into the ground with a roof of corrugated iron with earth heaped on top) and insisted that I go inside. In those days young people did as they were told so I reluctantly went and sat at the far end where lots of people were sheltering. After a short while, the man responsible for me being there, shouted that planes were overhead, and he was very agitated, standing at the entrance, when there was an almighty crash and that end of the shelter caved in. He was the only casualty, and I can only assume there was no blast, and wonder if one of the slave labourers employed by the Germans had forgotten to put the explosives in the bomb that hit the shelter. I gave up on the evening out and went back home. The next day my mother told me she had heard everyone was killed in the shelter which was in our road, but I know the only casualty was that Good Samaritan."

SPITFIRE

Grief, Fear and Anxiety

Isabel explained that when her father was called up, her mother suffered very much.

"My mother's illness, resulting from an over active thyroid gland, reasserted itself with panic attacks and agoraphobia. We had slept in the same bed since my father's call-up and I was sometimes woken up by the shaking of the bed, and would sit by it, holding my mother's hands which were dripping with sweat, until she stopped shaking and could drink a cup of hot, sweet tea. Uncle Archie was one of three brothers, all in the Armed Forces. He arrived on leave just after the evacuation of Dunkirk. After the usual greetings when we came back from school, we were all intercepted by my mother and told us she had never seen a man in such a state, and he had cried like a baby. It was years before I discovered that only a few of his company of 120 men had returned, and he himself had collected 80 identity discs from hundreds of dead bodies on the way back to the beach. …was he a wimp, this uncle of mine, to have reacted so intensely to such an experience….he was to prove himself time and again in the Burma campaign? My Uncle Willie went down with his ship at the Anzio beach-head later in the war.(1944). My father was either in Sri Lanka or India by that time and it was terrible to think of my father getting the news of his brother's death, well after the event. Then there was the complication that Willie was announced `Missing, presumed killed,` which made my Aunt Lizzie hang onto a wholly unjustified hope for years on end."

Helen also recalls the trauma of families losing relations.
"In 1941 we had a cousin to stay for a few months. Her husband was missing in a submarine in the Mediterranean. She was pregnant and had a large Labrador, and her mother in Central London was unable to cope. So my mother looked after her. Eventually her husband was declared dead and she married a farmer older than her father, but had three more children. At roughly the same time we heard that our cousin from the same side of the family had been blown up and killed in a tank in Belgium. Soon after this my father's cousin, a sea captain on the Clyde in Scotland, went down with his boat. My

brother and I also sorely missed our younger siblings who were evacuated to North Wales."

My own parents must have kept their worries hidden, as although my brother was in the Navy, I never witnessed any particular anxiety on their part, though I do remember Mother's joy whenever she received a blue air mail from him from somewhere unnamed. All the contents were severely censored, so I don't think they brought any news about where he was or what he was doing, but at least we knew that at the time of writing, he was alive. When he came home on leave he told them more of course, though even then he had to be careful, as in those days we were told that "walls have ears."

People mostly seem to have a built in belief that they will survive, however much evidence there is to the contrary.

"At seventeen I decided to join friends living in Highbury, London, and saw the effects of the buzz bombs and rockets launched from Germany but felt I was indestructible so never felt much fear."

Two of Watson's uncles were in the army. "The elder became frustrated because he remained in England and volunteered to become a Bevin Boy working in the coal mines, where he stayed till the end of the war. The other was trained for the D Day invasion, reaching Normandy in a landing craft on the second day. Years later, he told me that as they approached the beach, he and his friends thought they had little chance of surviving the bombardment. In the event all he suffered was the loss of a front tooth from hitting the helmet of the man in front when the craft shuddered to a halt. He was in a battalion that fought its way through France and Belgium and into Germany, ending the war unscathed and returning home to a celebration organised by the family in the local Co-op hall."

Strangers

Brenda,
"We had two officers billeted with us, a Mr. J, and a very glamorous Captain, who had an affair with the daughter of a local big wig."

"Because of parents being out a lot, we had living in help in the house, namely Ada. She had lived as a help in a clergyman's house and she joined the rather noisier environment of our family. She remained until old age! She never learned to read or write or answer the telephone, but she became devoted to the family and learnt a lot of cooking from my mother by just watching and copying."

"We were fortunate to have a maid for the largish house, 5 bedrooms. We constantly had evacuees from London knocking at the door, asking if we could put them up. We ended up having a single lady who worked at the RAF hospital laboratory nearby. We could keep our maid on only if we took in homeless people escaping from the bombing. The laboratory lady counted as one of these."

Peter Gillard. remembers the bond which sprang up between himself and other boys, with older men in the village, who could explain the war to them and give them some kind of feeling of security.
"Ex WW1 men acquired a certain glamour and morbid fascination for us lads, especially if ex-officers –as this class found itself in charge of the Home Guard platoons. Mr. Lile was in the Home Guard and had the unenviable task of guarding the only line of electricity pylons (very small ones) in the neighbourhood."

Strangers seemed to be everywhere, and talked a foreign language in many cases.
"Our next excitement was at the fall of France, when the parks were full of exhausted servicemen lying on the grass in bright sunshine while local volunteers went round with tea and cigarettes. My school playing grounds were filled with French servicemen who were locked in while they decided

whether to return to their occupied country, or fight on. One young man tried to talk to me, but my French was very hesitant and I couldn't understand. I asked the French mistress what "Voulez vous jigajig" meant, and she said it was not used in polite society!"

Members of the armed services were given hospitality by those living near their bases.
"We had the aerodrome at Meir and had been to events called Empire Day events.
Someone in our road organised rotas for inviting the RAF personnel to visit us in their off duty times. We had a good looking trainee pilot. I wonder if he survived the war. I made him a little wool golly for good luck, also had a ground crew chap called Bert Harwood. His parents lived in Portsmouth and had a very bad time in the bombing there."

By having to share their lives, people came to understand and help those people with whom they would not normally mix.
Marion remembers her dad's scheme to "supplement his income and dodge the evacuees, by renting the first floor of our house to a woman pharmacist whose husband was a wireless operator in the merchant navy. It turned out well, except one day the husband turned up on the front step, with a bundle of clothes under his arm, looking haggard. `I've been torpedoed.` he said. `Is the wife in?` Mum brought him in, fed him, sent him up to his bed, then rang the pharmacy to tell his wife. She came home to find him `sleeping like a baby,` and came down to talk to mum and tell her of her fears about him He was a nice man, with a sense of humour, and we missed him when he was torpedoed for the second time and never returned."

Peter Gillard remembers the very special kindness and sense of humour which the British people can show towards strangers. "The coming of the Americans was a huge event. To prepare for D Day a school of Combined Operations was established at Fremington. This was a big affair and much of the North Devon beach features, as well as the estuary, were used for training purposes. British and American youthful soldiers would come into Barnstaple, and Father, concerned for their moral well-being would have them up to the house for tea and a chat. Obscure inventions to breach the `Atlantic Wall` the German defences on the Northern France coast, were tested on the beaches at Instow among the strictest security. Father was part of this protective screen, but the public still gathered and watched some spectacular failures of some devices, accompanied by impressive explosions as the inventions trundled up the beach, became stuck in the sand, toppled over and blew up!

There was a joke going round at the time, in that when Eisenhower came to visit the School of Combined Ops, as it was called, he asked specially if he could have a pint of that `famous English bitter`. In the pub, he was given a pint, which he is alleged to have sipped and told the bar man to `pour the bloody stuff back into the horse, it`s flat`. This was an allusion to `horse piss` of course. A rustic voice in the corner spoke up and told Ike that `of course it's flat, the beer has been waiting for you for three years!` An allusion to the Americans' late entry into the war."

For many of the children, strangers in the home spelled more fun. Peter Gillard shows this in his story. "Father had a friend stationed in Barnstaple for a time early in the war. He used to go riding with my Father, regularly falling off. He was a nice man rather lonely, with a stock of very corny jokes. One was, `Open the window and let me throw out my chest`. If frustrated or a bit fed up, he would prowl around saying `Unk-a-Dunk` many times. He gave Mother a good deal of amusement.

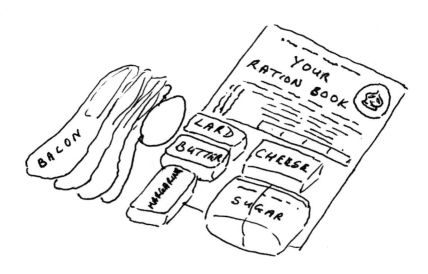

Censoring and Propaganda.

It is amazing how used we became to having no information, and having to rely on rumour. The media must have been well schooled in a way that seems hardly credible today. Our writers describe this.

Brenda says;
"No one had any idea that radar was being developed in Malvern, there were so many hush hush posters like `Walls have ears`, and `Be like Dad, keep Mum.` and the ubiquitous `Careless talk costs Lives.`"

Peter Gillard points out the dark side of rumour
"People suspected anyone with a faintly German name. Mr. Spiegalhalter, a Barnstaple resident since the days of Queen Victoria, was regarded (shamefully), with some suspicion, but he carried on blithely, and the idea fizzled out. One, Mr. Strauss, taught at the Grammar school, he was a nice man, and wrote mother a very kind letter when father died, which was more than anyone else did. On the topic of rumours, opportunistic lads would tell harassing and impossible tales (as a change from their opinions on sex) of finding dead or dying German airmen in shot down planes on their farms. No one but the most impressionable believed them! There were far more local rumours than reality, such as U boats in Barnstaple Bay, parachutists on Exmoor."

Perhaps this is an appropriate place to mention the place schools had in engendering patriotism in children. Of course patriotism was a part of the societal psyche, anyway, but the fact that we were taught to sing such songs as "There'll always be an England and England shall be Free" shows how teachers did their bit to reinforce our attitudes. Peter Gillard remembers a humorous aside about this song. The second line of it was `The Empire too, What does it mean to you?` Peter says "My hearing even then was not perfect and I thought the word was `Empatoo.` I thought this was some kind of red, white and blue parrot."

"U. Boats in Barnstaple Bay?!"

Entertainment

There was dominance of News programmes over all other, a state of affairs which has persisted till today. As Peter Bruce recalls:

"News was listened to at least twice a day. Children's programmes were generally daily and in fact Radio was a constant in our lives except when there was no electricity. The gramophone was played almost every day, especially in the school holidays."

The radio was vitally important to everyone and board games and reading were alternative ways of spending evenings round the fire, usually the only source of warmth in the house. I know in our house, there was competition to get the seats nearest to the fire, except when Mum and Dad were around, as they were then given pride of place. However hard you tried, and however much you built up the fire, if you could get spare wood or coal, there was always a draught across the back of your legs, owing to the fact that open fires suck in cold air, to heat it up, and this causes a cool wind to blow continually across the floor, to feed the fire.

Helen describes family entertainment.

"The wireless was a constant in our lives, except when there was no electricity. The gramophone too was played almost every day, especially in the school holidays. Children's` programmes were generally daily, and Forces Favourites on a Sunday. Humour was a regular, e.g. Tommy Handley, Arthur Askey, Richard Murdoch, and Wilfred Pickles. Music…Workers Playtime came from different factories each morning. We had a young lady, Florence, for a while to help in the house. She had had two fingers blown off in the munitions factory at Radway Green and could no longer do that work. She loved popular music and would carry a small radio, plugging in to whichever room she was in and she`d sing along as she worked. My brother loved her. Wartime songs had many catchy tunes, and are still sung today. Vera Lynn has worn well across the years. I had a parallel agenda for the gramophone i.e. Bizet´s L´Arlesienne Suite, Barber of Seville and many other popular classics. The Potteries have long had a good musical tradition and mother always encouraged us with piano lessons and later with visits to concerts.

In the long winter evening there was plenty of time for family "board games", though father was often out working and William not enthusiastic. He liked to have a long-drawn-out game of monopoly with one friend which would carry on for more than one session. I think our favourites were Halma and Lexicon.

So far I have omitted reading, which was probably the most time consuming and influential of our hobbies. Richmal Crompton`s `William` went into wartime life and I read every word as soon as it was published. It was William's gang that encouraged me to start my own gang and several of the dubious tricks he played on people were copied. Arthur Ransome was another great favourite.

Enid Blyton was not disparaged. The Secret Garden and the Louisa M. Alcott books were all lapped up with Cervantes, Dickens and countless others. The cinema was attended nearly every week and war films were very popular e.g. Charlie Chaplin as Hitler, Leslie Howard as Pimpernel Smith, Shirley Temple in Bluebird and the Little Princess.

For this period of 1940-42, though the war was intensifying, as a family we were all under one roof and that type of stability prevailed, which many of our contemporaries were not able to enjoy. I think it was this period that helped to give me resources to cope with the big change to boarding school in Sept 1942."

Marion also describes the morale raising efforts of the B.B.C.

"The B.B.C. employed comedians who helped us see the funny side, old music hall artists returned, such as Rob Wilton, taking fun out of himself as he represented the average little harmless, ineffectual Englishman, just trying to cope. Arthur Askey was another I remember, but of all people who kept our morale up and raised our fighting spirit it was William Joyce, the Irishman who broadcast from Germany in an affected upper-crust English voice, trying to break our morale. He made a big mistake of sneering at the Royal Family, for many people liked them. British people were not revolutionary . He actually had the nerve to say our Queen was `dumpy.` Now this, for Mum (who was no royalist) was considered rude, ungentlemanly and horrid. Every time `Lord Haw Haw broadcast, she tuned in and shouted at the same time, at the wireless, `Liar!` `Sneerer` ----`Don't you dare come over here!` and such like things which got me going, so I was battle ready if any Germans came over to invade! The radio provided vital entertainment when there was no way of getting to a theatre or cinema. Plays, talks, and concerts kept our cultural life going, and it also aimed to educate us with children's` programmes, and brains-trusts."

Besides listening to `ITMA` and `Children's` Hour` which were regular wireless programmes, there were weird stations on the wireless set, like Rugby, Daventry, and Hilversum, and many others which filled me with a sort of reverent awe.

The war brought a special bit of fun for Brenda and her sister. There was a link trainer for the contingent of the Fleet Air Arm which was stationed nearby. This trainer was fitted up like an aeroplane, to teach men how to fly. As the Captain of this contingent was a friend of the family, he gave the two girls a treat, allowing them to have a go. "Virginia and I had a go. If you pushed the joystick too quickly, you got into a spin. I did."

"No 3
Mount St."

Games and Sport

Peter Bruce describes a favourite pastime of the lads.

"(Those bombs) caused no fatal casualties and only minor damage to property. After the raids we boys would go hunting for shrapnel. I remember on one occasion finding an almost complete bomb in Burslem cemetery. I had a bicycle and along with friends, after school or during holidays, we would visit the local areas where bomb damage had occurred both out of morbid curiosity and in the search for shrapnel.

Dad at this time, was an Air Raid Warden. This entitled him to have a tin hat, a special forces issue gas mask, his name on the gate, and a government issue stirrup pump. Buckets of water and a stirrup pump appeared to me at that time to be a passport to Nirvana. Along with friends we would take it out of the shed when Mother was not about, and stand by the front gate to squirt water over other children offering to fight any one who complained.

Although there were no holidays, events at holiday times were organised in the parks, and there were cricket matches between good scratch teams. One time there was a large crowd of spectators and a Lancaster bomber came down, across the playing area, somehow managing to miss the crowd and the team; nobody in the crew was injured. ..still the most amazing experience I have ever witnessed.

We used to go to Trentham on the bikes and then one of us would hire a boat, and row it round to some secret spot, where the rest would get in, discreetly beyond the gaze of the attendants, row around in it all day, then park up, and climb over the wire fence then back home on the bikes. A very cheap and entertaining day out! One of the attractions was gazing in wonder at the German prisoners who were incarcerated at Trentham park.

Because of lack of traffic, we used to play street games, e.g. Rounders, may I, peggy, cricket and football, using lamp posts and gates as wickets and goalposts.

Because of the use of horse drawn carts, we could hang on the back of the float. The roundsmen eager to get home, would gallop back , and we would have a thrilling ride, and be off out of the way, before the driver could get us with his whip. We had one comic a week, not always the same one because newspaper rationing meant that they only came out once a fortnight. By swapping around with my friends I could read them all including, as I got older, those with fewer pictures and more adventure stories. There were also second hand comics to buy for only a half-penny each.

We played cards, ludo, dominoes, shove halfpenny, and other table games we invented ourselves, and I collected stamps. The cinema played a very important role in our lives, there were six cinemas, three large, which showed up to date films for several days at a time, and smaller ones which showed cowboy films and comedies, starring, for instance, Charlie Chaplin. There were also theatre productions, which we used to watch from the Gods, and we amused ourselves by throwing things over the edge or spitting on our elders and betters far below. From up there, the performers looked like midgets. The pantomimes we went to were magnificent spectacles of colour and wonder to us children."

Dot, who came from a very large family, remembers the games they all used to play.

"There was never enough room in our house to sit down, so we had to be outside – in all weather and that's where we had our fun, jumping doffies (dares) off trees, playing in Jenko`s fields and in Northwood Park. My brothers were caught playing football on Jenko`s fields (which were pastureland). The police were called in by the farmer, and my Mother was fined 5 shillings. You can imagine the trouble they were in."

Maybe she would have had the same experiences even if there had not been a war on, but I gathered from her that it was lack of supervision, due in part to the adults being so busy, that allowed the children to get into scrapes.

Another writer lived on the edge of the country

"with fields all around us, it was really black in the blackout, but good for seeing the stars, especially shooting stars. Trenches were dug in the field at the back of our house, we had a great time playing in them. Dug in a connecting box pattern, they were great for playing hide and seek, and sliding down the earth piles left after digging, covered with snow in winter."

Helen talks about lack of supervision and all the fun they had growing up.

"The school holidays provided time to develop our "gang" activities, such as cycling certain distances in time trials, and going up the hill in Queens Rd with no hands on the handlebars - quite wrong nowadays. But we did get about the countryside to Trentham, Barlaston Downs, Hanchurch Woods and father afield, without our parents worrying. We climbed trees and made camp. I think Arthur Ransome helped us negotiate the island on Trentham Lake. Our rowing became quite proficient. The 4 oz of sweets per week seemed to satisfy us. We used to buy Dandelion and Burdock with our pocket money and often take picnics out for the day. While cycling, if there happened to be a convoy of American soldiers passing, they would throw out packets of Camel cigarettes from their vehicles. I didn't know how old they thought we were. I just passed them on to William, who unknown to parents, was a juvenile smoker.

At boarding school, there were changes in the sporting activities because of the war. The swimming pool had been taken over by Canadian soldiers and part of the playing fields were dug up to grow vegetables. Because of lack of transport, there was little inter-school sporting activity. However I took all games seriously and tried very hard in the inter-house age-group matches and sport has remained a lifelong interest. We did manage to visit our Grandmother in Hertfordshire, and also Wiltshire, where my Aunt Alice lived. At both places we met older cousins and friends in the Forces and heard tales of recent events in the war. At Granny's house, we heard the V1 bombs for the first time. They didn't come to Stoke. At Aunty Alice's there were several members of the Women's Royal Naval Service, with my cousin Barbara and her brother Chris all sleeping on hammocks, and friends from Tidsworth. For a few hours folk forgot the war and enjoyed themselves. We got to know soldiers from the barracks opposite our house. Twice we met our second cousin, who was a Major in the American Army.

We were very proud to have him coming in a jeep and thrilled to have a ride in it on another occasion, over Salisbury plain."

Rhona sums it all up.

"Because of meagre resources, we had to "make do" and be happy with simple pleasures. My mother would take us swimming at the local reservoir, or river, and picnics were enjoyable – I cannot remember a restaurant meal, cinema was a special treat. We played outdoors mostly, hide and seek , catching newts in our pond, fishing in the reservoir. Indoors we would read, do puzzles, play games, do drawing and painting and of course fight between ourselves! There were 2 boys of our age nearby and we would often play with them."

I remember the joy of being by the sea, and having long days without any adults around. The explosives factory which my father managed was built on the sandy shore line near Llanelli. The whole beach was out of bounds to everyone, as it had been classified as an area on which German ships might deliver German troops to invade us. It was defended by long rolls of barbed wire, and was said to have been covered with mines. However no one believed the story about mines, and we children began to bathe regularly off the beach after the first scare of invasion had passed. I don`t know if my mother and father were aware of this. We would crawl through the barbed wire, and then we were free, with the whole beach to ourselves, to frolic in the waves and race about on the sands. One day my friend Marjorie and I went down to the beach with my Aunt, and, leaving her with our towels, we rushed off to the waves. When we came back we saw her talking to a tall, broad man, in dark blue uniform. It was a coast guard, or someone else in authority, and he was giving my aunt, a plump lady of 67, with a broad cockney accent, a proper grilling. We should not be here, and the offence was so dire, he was going to march us all off of the police station. He asked us for our identity cards. My friend cheekily answered that we had no pockets in our swimming costumes, that is why we weren't carrying the cards. He relaxed, and let us off with a caution, no doubt seeing the humour in the situation. I sometimes wonder what a Nazi SS man would have made of the affair. No doubt he would have relaxed too, so long as we both had flaxen curls. I am surprised that Auntie was so easygoing with us, as it was possible that there were some mines there, even though we had believed the stories about mines were just made up, in order that the spies which we all believed were all around us, could pass on the news to the Germans.
I can't recall if we ever went swimming there again. Now the area is a country park, and even the ruins of the two Ordnance factories which were built there in the two wars, have long ago returned to the flora of bracken and the fauna of rabbits.

Rationing and Economies

Rationing meant that meals were boringly the same, unless you were the lucky person to know a farmer, or someone who had managed to smuggle a little bit from the ships coming into port, and you didn`t care about paying black market prices.

Peter Bruce obviously didn`t feel that rationing meant starvation.
"We had dinners at school, and as a wartime school boy, I thought the dinners were delicious. Great helpings of stew, sausage and mash, liver or roast, always followed by either a steamed pudding or rice pudding. Second and third helpings were available."

How different his descriptions are from the memories of the children who were at boarding school!

He goes on: "Clothes were also rationed and there was a flourishing black market in clothing coupons, the going rate being about £1 per book. One of my father's brothers would come and visit us on a Sunday, and cigarettes, coupons and money would soon change hands."

The arrival of the Americans in Britain made a difference to the food available to those people who had a lot to do with them, as in the case of Peter's father and thus, his family. His father was a musician and played at dances at their local American bases, as he describes:

"The Yanks were a happy go lucky and generous bunch. They were reputed to have banquets at their dances, and Dad used to come home with tins of American bacon. After all these years I can still smell it cooking, and we used to dip our bread into the sizzling fat. By getting hold of these supplies, Dad was able to swap some of them as barter for other things."

Home grown fruit was not rationed, nor was bread till after the war. The weekly rations depended partly on the success of the Merchant Navy to run the gauntlet of the Nazi U boats. The meat ration per week was the equivalent of one small chop, and a quarter of a pound of liver, plus two pence worth of corned beef. Sausage was not rationed but consisted mainly of fat and bread. Bacon, butter, cheese, margarine and sugar allowance went as low as two ounces per person per week. Most tinned foods were in very short supply and allocated on the points system, which meant one didn`t necessarily ever get them, and chocolates and sweets were limited to two ounces per week. There was also a zoning system which meant that people in North Staffordshire were never able to purchase confectionery manufactured in the South of England. Mars Bars, Milky Ways, and Maltesers were nearly unavailable, and milk chocolate disappeared to be replaced by a dark unappetising two ounce block of what was called "ration chocolate."

Marion speaks for all of us when she says "What you haven`t had, you never miss, so they say, and I didn`t miss having sweets, fizzy lemonade, crisps, ice-cream, nor did I miss having comics and soft toilet paper. The paper we used was cut up newspaper, cut up into squares (one of my jobs) and threaded through a string, and hung up in the toilet. If there were any photos of the enemy,- say Hitler, Mussolini, Goering, we especially enjoyed using them – I did anyway."

I personally do remember longing for the end of the war so we could have proper toilet paper again, and soap for the washing up.
Peter Gillard. remembers the wartime soap. "Saving up of odd bits of soap

was considered the right thing to do. The fragments could be heated up and moulded into a new bar. There were no detergents as we know them today. `Elbow Grease` was the order of the day. Soap was available for toilet purposes in limited quantities. There was also 'carbolic' soap, for more robust personal cleansing. Large bars of greenish soap could be bought and cut up into lengths, or pared into flakes to ease the washing of clothes. There was even a rugged soap which contained small grit, for the most hard scrubbing activities, whether floor or personal cleanliness."

Also I longed to be able to go into Woolworths and find a comb for sale. These things seem so ordinary and unimportant now, that it is almost impossible to imagine how the loss of them can affect one's ordinary life. I remember that Mother gave each of us girls a pound of jam to take back to school with us. I tried to make this pound of jam last me for the whole thirteen weeks. However thrifty I was and however thinly I scraped it on, it would only last a month. After that there was nothing to put on the sliced bread which was the mainstay of our last meal of the day, tea. We would have a small amount of sugar for our tea, and some of us would use this for the bread. My mother gave me a shilling a week pocket money, partly to buy stamps to write home. I did manage to get my ration of chocolate which amounted to a Mars Bar every week. My friend would also buy a Mars Bar, but she would eat hers all at once, then persuade me to give her some of mine. Because of this I learned very early in life that one slice of Mars Bar is actually quite sufficient, and when my own children wanted chocolate, they never obtained more than a slice from me.

Brenda was at boarding school, and her memories of rationing are positive. "I remember the food being excellent; the headmistress thought the cook was one of the most important members of staff. At home, Brenda says, "the back garden was dug up and we grew potatoes, we kept hens, they smelled and pecked each other."

My own memory of school food was that there was never enough of it. I gave up having milk in tea, because the jug was always empty by the time it got to me. Our food was put on the table in dishes, and we were supposed to help our selves and then pass on the dish. For those last in line there was little left.

Dot remembers hardship and short rations because the men in the house had to be fed well doing the hard work which they did. She says:

"There wasn't always enough for children, even with the rationing, as if there were heavy manual workers in the family, they got the children's rations. Father worked hard down the pit, and mother made sure that the ones who worked got fed properly. Us younger kids were the last in the queue, for food and clothing. The clothing coupons were used up by the workers, and we had their cast offs. There were no raincoats, of course, so when we went to school in all weathers, we were wet through." Hers was a very tough life, and she vowed her own children would not have to suffer as she had.

Isabel wrote also about privation and the efforts they had to make as children to get food. She says: "A lower standard of nutrition was something we also had to accept. The rations, often trumpeted as exemplary in terms of essential needs, were minimal and left out of the equation e.g. things that were no longer in ready supply, like tomatoes, oranges, bananas.

Our flat looked out onto a circle of shops and one day we witnessed a delivery of tomatoes to the greengrocer, kept by two old ladies. A queue gathered immediately, and we joined it. If you hesitated, the exotic item would be gone. We were amazed when at 12.30, the ladies locked up the shop, saying they would be open again at the usual time, two o'clock. Not wanting to lose our advantage, we stayed put for the long hour and a half. Finally my turn arrived, and the old lady explained that she was giving people a quarter of a pound of tomatoes. In our case this was a single tomato, but because she knew there were five people in our family, she had made sure it was a big one. Put to the test, and to my amazement, it did stretch, cut thin, over five slices of toast, and was much enjoyed with salt and pepper.

As the war went on, we became used to not finding in the shops the things on the list – outside of rations. I went a mile and a half one day, on a tip off that a greengrocer had raspberries. I tried five greengrocers without a single raspberry, and came home with a packet of Jacobs Creams, a pound and a half of rhubarb, and long, stiff, salted fish.

Early in the War, mother was seeing my father off at Waverley station, the first step in his Eastern posting, and saw an open carriage filled with fresh fish. There was a porter standing by and she asked where they were bound for. "Oh," he said airily,"They`re bound for London. Sometimes we get some back, if there`s any left at the end of the week. Have a couple." We could not begrudge sustenance to the people of London who were being bombed time and again, as we were not, nor could we begrudge anything to the armed forces who were risking life and limb, but I did think a little harder, when my mother`s younger brother came on leave from the Navy, and she offered him an egg for breakfast pretending we'd just had a half dozen after what had been, in fact, a five week famine. `Oh, don't offer me eggs!` he said. `I'm sick of them, we can have them any time- up to four at a meal.`

Rationing was so rigid that we almost didn`t dare court humiliation by returning an adulterated pot of marmalade. In it we found first a long hair, then a button, then a piece of glass. By that time my mother had had enough and sent me back with it to the Co-op, but while I was waiting at the counter, my basket tipped over, and the jar smashed. The manager (complete with bow tie) was called in to arbitrate on this important situation, and said, without much regret, that it could not be replaced, but when I opened the sticky paper, showing the button and the glass as evidence, he changed his mind and added in something unexpected (`off the ration` as the phrase had it) to make up.

Our budgie was a more serious casualty of war conditions. WE were all able to make do with dried egg and black bread, but the substitute bird seed, which was all we could get for Budgie, turned her beak black and induced fits. We managed to revive her twice with brandy, but one morning we found her on her back in the cage, stone dead with her little, twiggy claws in the air. We were often left in some confusion as to how exactly our actions were helping the war effort. Mother would apply precious butter or margarine to the feet of birds rescued from the tarmac in hot summer weather. She was also not above the usual confidence trick of placing a bowl in the middle of the table, into which we were invited to put the sugar which we would have had in our tea, in order to help the Finns. She always looked a bit vague, when we pressed her on how it would help them. She got off with this, but pushed her luck when she pressed my young sister to eat up her crusts for the same reason. At this Moira gave her permission to send them to the Finns if she really thought it would help.

Gardens were given over to vegetables and it was usual to see ranks of cabbages where once had been stretches of green lawn, edged with bright borders."

Watson`s memories are more positive:

"There may well have been profiteering during the war, but I don't remember hearing much about it. Rationing of food was seen as fair and seemed to work well. My mother was an excellent cook and, having had little money to spare before the war, very resourceful. Certainly, I never remember being hungry. My father still had friends who sold food but he would have regarded it as unacceptably disloyal to have bought in the Black Market. I remember on one occasion he was given a small lump of bacon as a present that he felt unable to refuse. It was carefully sliced and lasted for a few breakfasts but I saw that my father remained uncomfortable and took little pleasure in eating it. A British Restaurant was established in a neighbouring church hall where I remember eating with my parents. My memory is that the food was good but I don't think we went there on more than a few occasions, maybe because it didn't function for long."

In fact British Restaurants did last for several years, Watson must have been unlucky .

As Isabel said, to get enough food could be an arduous and sometimes unsuccessful task.

"Owing to Mother's illness I had to do the shopping, and soon daily milk deliveries were stopped at times because of a lack of man power. This meant that I had to use my lunch hour to walk the half-mile to the Co-op with empty bottles, and back with five pints of milk."

Most of our writers remember the lengths people went to in order to supplement the diet, and "recycle," in modern language – not to save the planet, but to help out in the general War Effort. Peter Gillard recalls:"At home we were expected to garden and Father had access to an allotment on a farm which had once belonged to the family. Salvage was ardently gathered, supervised by my Mother`s Mother, a widow, who lived with us. Newspapers etc were tied up in bundles and left out for the `ash cart`. Ash from fires was the main rubbish material in those days as packaging was almost non-existent, as we know it today. We had four grape vines by the house. The surplus grapes I would take down to the North Devon Infirmary, (Entirely Supported by Voluntary Contributions.) Here, blue clad war wounded would be nursed back to health and sit out by the river. Incidentally, the Voluntary Contributions in those days came largely from the mainly very public spirited local aristocracy and upper middle class folk."

Peter notes that the railings were all removed for the war effort, but the "superb wrought iron gates to the old Theatre were saved and became the entrance gates to a local 'important person's drive!' Just another twist in the story about what we all did to help the War effort, or to improve our conditions."

In my own family, my father kept pigs on spare ground near the house. We fed them on swill from the factory canteen, and a lot of the work was done by my father. When they were of age, they had to be slaughtered and all the pork was supposed to be sent into the general store of food to be rationed out among all. But I have to confess that one of the pigs, one day, mysteriously found its way into our outdoor lavatory and came out dead, to be singed in our back yard, cut up in our kitchen, and then made into bacon for our own family's consumption! We ate some of it when my brother came home on leave from one of his Naval assignments (whether in a Russian Convoy or the Med, I don`t know). I remember it was all done at dead of night, when we wouldn`t be spied upon. There were no neighbours living anywhere near the factory, and only the workers going on or off shift might have heard the poor pig complaining briefly at being locked in the lavatory. I am sure he was killed humanely by my sister, a medical student. Anyway, the bacon was marvellous.

Peter Gillard. has a pig story too. "Our neighbour had a small-holding on which he used to rear a couple of pigs. These were slaughtered at Christmas and I and my brother would go round and help `salt in` the pork for storage in huge jars, or `cloams`. We would have a big joint to take home with us afterwards. There were `war rations` available in the form of barley meal, for someone keeping a pig or chickens. The pig rations would be supplemented by stale loaves and boiled up waste vegetables and scraps. The rule was that `all swill must be boiled for an hour` to prevent the spread of infections."

We also kept hens and rabbits in our garden, and we had two chickens in particular, which we kept for two years, and in that time they each produced an egg every day for the two years. Then the fox got them. I used to sing to them every day, when home from school. The song was `Hey, little hen, when,

when, when, will you lay me an egg for my tea?` I don`t know who sang to them when I was away at boarding school, but they just kept laying, anyway.

Georgina questions the modern attitude about rationing.
"Everyone tells you now that rationing led to a healthy and adequate diet as no doubt it did, but adolescents growing fast were jolly hungry a lot of the time."
She also explains how her family eked out the rations. "Word of offal at the butchers would get round and everyone raced there to queue – it was off ration. That's the only time I have eaten sweetbreads, and very delicious they were. Sweets were rationed and children had more than adults; the bliss of a bar of blended chocolate was glorious! Rations were increased at Christmas, but one year, despite mother's best efforts the pudding turned out very pale, to her mortification."

Children at day-school sometimes found the food better than what they normally had at home. Not so Marion who says, "For the first time I sat down to school dinners -horrible mixtures of beet-root and mince, or fatty meat floating in thin, tasteless gravy. And the sweets, which many kids from a distant, poor housing estate thought were wonderful, were absolutely tasteless –rainbow pudding which was stodge with coloured stripes, or oversweet `treacle tart,` which wasn't treacle but syrup. No fruit ever to be seen, though apple trees grew around. At home we had eggs from our own hens, and vegetables from what had been our front lawn, but was now put down to produce and was called `the allotment` by Dad. Mum went to another green-grocer who had some oranges. When the three oranges were opened, one was bad and I was sent back, only to get an earful from the woman who ran the shop. `Tell your mother it's not MY fault. I can't see inside the oranges`. Butter was what most people missed, but Dad knew a chap at work, who liked margarine better than butter, so we used to swap our margarine ration for his butter ration! We had little money to buy clothes, so we swapped clothing coupons with a farmer for butter, as his daughter wanted a new outfit. Mother picked, and pressed, and enlarged or re-cut clothes, making hobble skirts from Dad`s old trousers, and unpicking yards and yards of wool from old jumpers, washing and skeining it, and then re-knitting."

I still remember one of the dresses my mother made from two of her old dresses. The bodice was dark red, with a heart shaped neckline. The skirt was brown. I felt marvellous in it, and other girls were really envious. I was aged thirteen and can imagine what kind of reception a present of such a garment would elicit from a modern teenager. (Of course, in those days, there were no teenagers. We were all children, until we were fourteen, when we became adults, with jobs, unless we went on to study.)

We also made sheets last longer, by turning them sides to middle. Peter Gillard remembers doing this chore, when he helped his grandmother by turning the handle on the sewing machine. "I would turn the handle, and did this very fast sometimes out of devilment. Granny Pearce would then remonstrate and that was rather a frightening experience. Though tiny, she packed a punch."

Boarding Schools varied as to the food provided. Brenda says:

"I remember the food being excellent at Lawnside in Malvern, where I was at school. Each month we had a jam list, you chose your one pot of jam or marmalade for the month and we each had our own small pot of butter, they were on shelves outside the dining room. You picked your own up as you went in to breakfast or tea.

At dinner parties at home the main course was broad beans and bacon (from rations) and parsley sauce, and sometimes it was sausage pie. Cousins in Australia sent us very welcome tins of sausage meat. By this time the maids and chauffeur-gardener had been called up, and we had an ex-gypsy who made superb pastry; we had grown out of nannies…one farmer gave my father a joint of pork, some butter, eggs and cream, which was absolutely illegal. He was stopped by a policeman going home, who asked him what he had in the car. Father took a deep breath and told the truth. The policeman clapped him on the shoulder, and said, `Don`t you wish you had! Drive on!`

Apart from ration books for food, we had clothing coupons and all clothes were utility, very skimpy with hardly any hem, but brides were allowed a few coupons. Derek`s bridesmaids had dresses made from old curtains.

Stockings were in very short supply, women painted their legs and managed to paint a line down the back of their legs, stockings were seamed in those days. My husband-to-be came back with nothing but a demob suit. Before he came back his Mother went into Henry Whites in Newcastle and bought two

shirts, the man put them on the counter and demanded coupons, she explained he was coming home after nearly five years away and would be bringing his coupons, the man refused to let her have the shirts, it was an attitude very prevalent. `Don't you know there`s a war on?` he asked.
Of course sweets were rationed, our parents gave us all their ration and we used to buy cough sweets."

Helen remembers some help from farmers. Her father was a doctor and the family profited from the gratitude of patients.
"We came to acquire some little "extras" to our rations, half a dozen eggs or a brace of pheasants, or some butter from farmer patients; quite unsolicited."

Rhona was a tall child, and she remembers rationing only too well. She says there were "very small amounts of butter, sugar, jam, meat, eggs, tea available, and this encouraged my mother to grow vegetables, and we two children had our own patch for leeks, broccoli, salads."

Helen remembers the shortage of fuel even though her father had a small petrol allowance for his important task of tending patients. For an adolescent girl, the shortage of clothes and cloth was a constant grievance.
"Petrol was severely rationed, so journeys were limited, and we bicycled everywhere. I carried my aunt's luggage to the station in a wheelbarrow, when there was no petrol. I cannot remember any local buses, and we lived half a mile out of town.
New clothes were scarce, and mothers altered and made new clothes out of old materials. Blackout curtains were usually homemade and were meant to exclude light from being seen by aeroplanes. When I went to boarding school at the end of the war, we bought 2nd hand uniforms, often altered in size to fit us – `old CLO` was the second hand uniform shop for parents with children at the school.
I cannot remember `shopping,` apart from queuing with my mother for food necessities.
We received 2 oz of sugar and 2 oz of butter per week. It was bad luck if you finished it before the end of the week. There didn`t appear to be a bread shortage, so if your butter could spin out you might manage two or three slices of bread per meal. Spam was popular at breakfast, but I hated porridge

and went without it if there was no cereal. Under the circumstances we were quite well fed. There was always a third of a pint of milk and a bun at break, and a cooked meal at lunchtime, and something to fill up with in the evening, at high tea. The children who suffered most were those from farming backgrounds who at home were used to unlimited eggs, cheese, butter, meat etc. rather than our meagre rations."

Peter Gillard lived in the country.

"Rationing was applied to us all. Granny would mix together the butter and margarine rations, cool them in the meat safe and then cut them up into little cubes, enough to last everyone the week. We could separate the cream from the milk and make a little butter, and occasionally get a pat of butter from a local farmer. Rationing and scarcities affected us far less than was the case in the big towns, and especially in the cities `up country.` Our proximity to the country side and Father's help which he gave to a local small holder assisted us."

Peter describes how important the old country skills were, which were practised by the expert country men, to support the city dwellers. "North Devon was a good source of protein for those living `up country`, even in London. Farming was very much the main industry and still is, and in those days, there were huge numbers of rabbits on the farms. Those huge Devon banks, between fields and lining the roads, were ideal burrowing and home-making sites for rabbits. These were caught by the thousands by tenant farmers and the income used to pay the rent; or, professional trappers were employed. In either case, the dead rabbits, in their thousands, were strung up on long poles, and hung in special, slatted railway wagons for `export` and sale, to city populations. Two or three such wagons would go off twice a week, at the back of a goods train.

Fish was easy to get in Barnstaple, The bay of the same name was a great source of fish, and thus there was a regular export of fish from the town. This went in an open wagon, covered and interleaved with ice. This wagon would be taken by rail. In its journey over the Taw, this train and its open fish wagon passed under a road bridge. A very naughty boy from Barnstaple Grammar School was caned severely for standing on the parapet of the bridge, and `peeing` into the open fish wagon as it passed beneath.

It was not unusual that a sheep would `accidentally` get shot, in mistake for something alien or during a `night firing exercise` by the Home Guard; later to be quietly cut up by a compliant butcher and sold surreptitiously on the black market. Later a University friend of mine from deepest Devon told me that this happened from the start of the war, when his father was made Captain of the local Home Guard. Incidentally the arms and ammunition for the village Home Guard detachment were kept under the floor boards of the farm's 'summer house'!"

"Business as usual — collecting empties, may be delayed"

Absence of family members and teachers.

Since Mother was working on war work at the factory, we girls looked after ourselves. Helen, five years my senior, cooked for us, and thus began her life interest in cooking. She also organised the house cleaning, in which I rather sporadically participated, and thus began a habit which I never lost. Otherwise we were completely free to please ourselves, whiling away the holidays with bike rides, walks, reading, painting and playing with the dogs. No TV in those days, and we only listened to the radio in the evenings. All of us used to tune in to Handley`s Half Hour, and ITMA It's That Man Again, long lasting soap operas about some staff in a block of offices. Tommy made a quick fire succession of more or less "clean" jokes. Dad used to laugh uproariously at some of the catch phrases which were repeated every programme, one being the famous "can I do yer now, sir," uttered by the cleaning lady when she went into the Manager's office to tidy up. I could never understand what Dad was laughing about, but Mother always used to expostulate "Dad," in a shocked tone when he started laughing at these and other phrases. It was years later before I realised that there was innuendo in the words. Most of the days were spent "mooching about" as recorded in my diary. Looking back I don't know what this mooching about amounted to, I just know we did it. Mother`s absence made me feel lonely, but also we could have a lot of freedom to please ourselves. As for Dad, working long hours, we actually saw more of him than we had before the war when he was working away from home. Whenever he was there, tending his chickens and rabbits, or his vegetable patch, late in the evening when he finally returned from work, he seemed the source of all excitement.

Many children had to make shift for themselves without the guidance and support of adults. All the adults worked very hard, and so not surprisingly, children growing up saw little of their parents.

Dot was one of these.
"We saw little of our Dad; he never gave us nothing, never talked to us, but we hadn't time to be depressed....One of our brothers, Albert, was in the

Navy. They all survived the war, but Albert was missing for 6 months after his submarine was torpedoed. Mother wrote to the war office and found that he was safe in America. There was no news, no communication."

Isabel was another.
"My father was away from us for about seven years, first in Ceylon, then India, and was not demobilised until several months after VJ day. This was an enormous strain on my mother, requiring her to be both mother and father to four lively children When I look at the carefree lives of my grandchildren, I see a big difference, mainly in the maturing process. They seem sophisticated beyond their years in some ways, but are without the heaviness of responsibilities that were laid on us. We had to grow up fast. They have been allowed to remain children.".

For Watson the absence of his Dad was minimal, but noticed by the youngster.
"For much of the time the war seemed far away although I remember always having to carry my gas mask in a cream coloured cylindrical can and my father spending nights away from home fire watching."

The population at home became lopsided, many more women than men, many more of the old and very old, and very few young men indeed.

This is described by Isabel.
"One hidden deprivation came from the call up of so many men and women as time went on – these would otherwise have been manning our primary and secondary schools and universities."
Lack of staff did not affect the very small children, as Local Authorities supported kindergarten care, to release mothers for war work.
Watson says.
"At the beginning of the war I started at elementary school, after which my mother went back to weaving in a cotton mill. Before and after school I attended a Play Centre organised in the school and I assume funded by the local authority so that parents could be in full-time employment for the war effort. It was run by a very kind and highly committed woman who went far beyond basic child minding in encouraging our learning and wider interests. The school itself was small with about 30 pupils in each year and what I

remember as good teaching. I was there throughout the war, going to the local Grammar School in the first year of the eleven plus in 1945.

Two of my father's brothers were in the army. The elder became frustrated because he remained in England and volunteered to become a Bevin Boy working in the coal mines, where he stayed till the end of the war. The other was trained for the D-Day invasion, reaching Normandy in a landing craft on the second day. Years later, he told me that as they approached the beach, he and his friends thought they had little chance of surviving the bombardment. In the event all he suffered was the loss of a front tooth from hitting the helmet of the man in front when the craft shuddered to a halt. He was in a battalion that fought its way through France and Belgium and into Germany, ending the war unscathed and returning home to a celebration organised by the family in the local Co-op hall."

SPIT FIRE

Living conditions

Most of our writers remember can remember being freezing cold during wartime winters. Those years seem in retrospect to have been grey as well as cold there being no paint and no painters to cheer things up. In our school we had a large playroom, but it was always very cold as the meagre coal ration allowed for insufficient heating. We spent most of the time when we were supposed to be playing, sitting on these radiators, but this was done surreptitiously, as it was forbidden, since it was supposed to result in chilblains. I did get chilblains, which were very painful and itchy, and, if they were scratched, fingers and toes became raw and bleeding. On Sunday nights we were allowed to sit in a wonderful warm room, where we sat on the floor round our house mistress, and did our mending.

The old Victorian buildings were large, and very cold, as well as gloomy, and the lavatories and cloak rooms were especially awful. There weren't enough cleaners, and certainly no plumbers to install new loos, which were ancient ones from the middle of the nineteenth century. They were so disgusting that I refused to go to them during morning school, and would wait till we got back to the house for lunch ....torture!

The house was very cold in winter, such heating as there was did not penetrate up to the bedrooms. Our room was over a covered car port with a flat roof and three outside walls. We six girls in the room shared one hot water bottle we would pass round, each having had it for about five minutes. By the time it came to me it was nearly cold, and I was nearly asleep, in spite of the cold. Rubber was in very short supply, and one couldn't buy hot water bottles.

Isabel remembers the few weeks while the school was shut, while shelters were being built at the beginning of the war, but with the winter came the return to school.

"When the cold became severe, we were back in school again. There were rather more women teachers than men. For me, cold became the main characteristic of the war period: One coal fire was not enough to heat a whole house, but it was all that anyone had by that time. Coal was rationed. We went to bed in winter with hot water bottles and woke with frost or ice on the inside of the windows. The woollen gloves, which we soon learned to knit for ourselves, were not proof against the worst weather and my feet seemed to be permanently frozen."

She writes in detail how to get dressed in the cold.
"We were always cold. Coal was rationed and was only enough to keep one fire alight, however big the house was. This meant that bedrooms were unheated and, although never kept awake by the cold we woke in winter to a thick coating of ice on the inside of the windows. Dressing was a feat of sheer invention ensuring that you never exposed an inch of flesh to the sub-zero temperatures flowing round you, if you could possibly help it. Knickers were pulled on under the protection of your nightgown. Stockings followed and feet were thrust into shoes in expectation of the cold layer of leather that even the wool of our school stockings could not fully disguise. Thus strengthened you took a deep breath, and held it while throwing off your night garments and pulling on your liberty bodice, blouse, gym-slip and cardigan. You were up. Nothing could touch you now. Until the walk to school that is. Fingers started aching with cold almost immediately and by the time you reached school your toes were in the same state......The memory of freezing cold as a keynote of wartime privation is still a strong memory."

Helen talks humorously about clothing and bathing.
"Living conditions were Spartan with 5 inches of water in the twice-weekly bath, a low temperature for the heating system and only such clothing as the coupon allowance permitted – very little mufti although there were people clever with the needle and thread. I remember one girl making a silk dress out of parachute silk obtained from a member of her family in the R.A.F. (reputedly from a Luftwaffe pilot who had bailed out"

I remember longing for the day when one could go into a Woolworth's and buy a new comb, and some soapflakes for washing dishes; or clothes. `When the war is over...`was a laboured phrase, prefacing every dream we had, even of doing such a simple job as washing hair or socks.

Family stress

Everyone tried to keep some normal pattern of life going.

In Helen's case this meant having days out every so often, in the school holidays.

"One holiday we had with mother was by train to stay by Rudyard Lake. We rowed and walked for nearly a week. As I see it now, mother tried hard to do the best for all of us and keep her work going, but it was not easy."

Her family also took holidays away, staying with relatives or friends.

"Another summer holiday nearby was a month on a farm in Cholmondeley. We knew the farmer´s sister well and she persuaded him to have William and me, as long as we did some work on the farm. It was great! I shared a bed with the elder daughter. There was only an outdoor toilet plus a "gazunda" in the bedroom. We helped as far as we were able with harvesting. William nearly got himself killed by an Army truck when he crossed a road from one field to another. We learnt first hand about the Land Army. There were two jolly girls on the farm who livened up the local labourers."

The difficulty of keeping things normal, was evident in this description of one mother's reaction on hearing of all the death and destruction going on.

"We did not know anyone affected by the bombings, or death, but had constant reminders of destruction of cities. My mother used to say `That is another child with no father, and a wife with no husband` and I think this was influenced by the terrible losses of the 1st World War when she was in her teens."

Adults suffered from stress and overwork, as Watson remembers.

"Up to the beginning of the war my father had sold green grocery, poultry and fish from a lorry in Haslingden, an East Lancashire cotton town. Too old to join the armed forces, he went to work in a local engineering factory that had previously made machinery for the local cotton mills but was now making aircraft parts. The pressure was intense with 12 hour shifts and after some months, the health of my father who had been invalided out of the First World War with a damaged heart, was deteriorating rapidly. Fortunately he obtained a job in the local Borough Treasurer's Office"

Brenda, who came from a well off family shows how even in her life, there was stress among the adults. She and her sister helped as much as they could to carry on the social life expected of her parents.

"Virginia and I used to wait on, if there were cocktail parties, we did not go to them, but we enjoyed helping when it was my mother's turn. My father was usually out working When he was there, if the party went on too long he would throw the coats into the room, turn the lights off and say `Party's over`"

Men faced uncertain futures, whereby they might have to leave home and family, as Peter Gillard shows.

"Father was expecting to be called up. This was a major worry, not only because of the danger to him and our potential isolation at home, but because several employees at `no. 25` (our business premises) had been drafted and there would have been no one to run the business. ….Father did not get called up because he got ill, the authorities realised he was badly needed to run the business. …he was enrolled as a special constable, and he had some difficult times when thus employed, especially when the Americans came in great numbers to the School of Combined Operations at Fremington, in preparation for D Day. Father would never let me see his police notebook, but I think he had some fairly unpleasant incidents to sort out. I do remember him saying that the `xxx Regiment` were among the most given to making trouble."

Sometimes it is difficult to sort out whether the attitude of adults was the result of the stress they were feeling because of the war, or for more constant worries e.g. poverty.

Since Dot's family had its three elder boys in the services, it is no wonder that the parents were stressed out, and in this case it was the children who might suffer.

"Father had enough wages to afford a proper Sunday dinner of roast meat, but still the children were bullied." But we must realise that the Victorian attitude towards children, which was that they should be seen and not heard, was still the norm among many families.

"We were constantly threatened with a clout for anything which caused money to be spent…money that mother hadn't got. Mother gave us a good hiding for joining a Sunday School, which was giving us parts in a little gospel play. The reason was not one of religion or principles, but because each attendance would cost her 3 pence. Mary got knocked down by Jenko`s horse one day when we were out playing. Her leg was hurt, but we didn`t dare go home. We went to Granma`s and she put some ointment on it, and she wrapped a man's scarf round it."

We were all schooled not to make a fuss, and for many older people that is a habit they have kept up.

What we knew about the war

Some children understood little of what was going on, unless there was enemy action in their neighbourhood. This was especially true of deprived children, they were hardly worse off, except for the air raids. Dot never knew the progress of the war.

"Your dad might listen to the boxing, your mum might listen to a play, we didn`t listen to the radio, as far as I know. My father had a paper every day, then it was used the next day to light the fire."

Some however, for instance, Isabel, "had a good grasp of what went on, and its significance. We were a family where things were discussed and answers were freely given to any questions we had. Things were pretty well spelt out in the news broadcasts. You could not fail to know that there were different theatres of war, and that things were going well or less well according to the tone of the broadcast. Sometimes you knew that reverses were being downplayed and could read between the lines and send your concentration in a in a particular direction.

Watson was a child who understood very much of the significance of the current events.

"My memory is that for most of the time most people followed the government line that hatred should be focused on the German Nazi leaders rather than the German population. The only enemy soldiers I saw were Italian prisoners standing on the back of an open lorry. One boy in our group shouted abuse but they didn't respond - presumably relieved to be out of the conflict.

My father was addicted to national and international news throughout his life and never more so than during the war. It was from listening to his reactions to the BBC that my political attitudes were formed. Those I remember most vividly were weekly broadcasts from Alexander Werth describing the battle for Stalingrad - legendary for its ferocity, sustained over months, and its crucial importance for the outcome of the war with Germany. This was a time when old antagonisms were set aside and Britain and the United States were sending planes and tanks via Arctic convoys, often at great cost in lives, ships and support aircraft, to aid the Soviet war effort. A recurring issue I heard debated was the timing of the Second Front, by a landing in France."

Helen also knew what was happening.
"There was access to the wireless and a newspaper (Daily Telegraph) in the house and I continued to take an interest in the progress of the war."

Marion is conscious that the B.B.C. vetted what was broadcast. "The B.B.C. kept us going. It kept us in touch with the news about the war (though did not tell us all the bad news.)" An example of the way news which brought down morale was not broadcast was when details of the tube disaster, when shelter seekers panicked and there was a fatal crush at Bethnal Green, in 1944. This news was not broadcast or publicised.

In my own case, we had to listen to the news over breakfast at school, from the age of ten, and I also kept a journal, complete with photographs collected from newspapers, about various war fronts and battles. I still have this.

Peter Gillard says that he knew little about the war. He knew when relatives and friends of the family were called up. "The daughter of a prominent chapel-goer joined the A.T.S. Sometime later in the war, she was sent to Italy where it was rumoured she smoked and drank and generally `lived it up`. This was a big worry as she came from a strict `Chapel` background. I can vividly recall the sinking of the `Hood`, which was reported in the headlines of the `News Chronicle`, (the paper for Liberals), which we used to take. Living where we did meant that war details were all somewhat second hand. News bulletins and the papers were a source, but there was no sense of immediacy. Father was not called up, as he had the family business to run and was short of staff anyway, including his brother. There were phrases which stick in my mind, heard over the wireless. One of these was the statement that `mopping up` operations were continuing. This occurred with greater frequency as the Normandy invasion gathered momentum. I could only relate `mopping up` to activities of a more household nature, in this context. War developments were also somewhat distant. Father gave up his horse riding; (he was a very good horseman,) to do his bit, bearing in mind he was not called up. He joined the Special Constabulary. This Police work was quite arduous, and he would come back from the business, and change into his uniform for duties at the Police Station. His main task was driving a huge Police Wolseley car round Exmoor with three other constables `looking for paratroopers.` None were ever found and I discovered later that many reports of parachutes seen billowing on the moors, as if just touching down, were actually sheep!"

Peter also tells a story about the very last months of the war. His uncle was stationed near the South coast, and he happened to look up, and there, very high and meteoric in its speed, he saw something trailing flame `rather like a flying lamp post`. It was heading North, travelling at huge speed, and he felt he had been one of the very few who actually SAW a V-2 rocket on its way to London - Hitler`s last throw in the aerial attack on London.

"I thought at first it was a lamp post."

Our personal War Effort and sacrifices

At boarding school we were taught to do all the usual make-do-and-mend tasks, skills which I have not forgotten, but seldom practise!
I learned how to darn the holes in my stockings, using a darning mushroom, and also how to sew on buttons, and how to knit squares, which were collected to make blankets for refugees and bombed out families.

Peter Bruce learned to garden too, a skill to be treasured throughout life.
"Our school had an allotment, and the vegetables for the school dinners were grown here by the boys who were considered to have learned all they could. The master would take us along in the morning, explain what had to be done, then leave us to it! When we had finished the task we would retire to the tool shed and smoke illicit Woodbines. Also we would live in bell tents, and help on neighbouring Staffordshire farms at harvest time. We would collect horse manure from the streets, and then take buckets of it to sell at the allotments. The gardeners would give us rhubarb to eat. We were lucky if we got sugar to cook it with, but otherwise we would eat it unsweetened. If we didn't get it given us, we would remember where it was growing, then come back and help ourselves."

My own little war effort was to collect money for the Red Cross, by washing other childrens' socks for a few pence a pair, a rate much lower than would have been charged by the laundry. I earned 18s one term, and my friend and I received a letter of thanks from some important person in the organisation.

Isabel remembers gardening as well as other skills she learned.
"Dig for Victory was a slogan put before us constantly. In spite of opposition from our neighbours, who wanted more than their share, we took over part of the village common land behind our house, to cultivate. In the end my brother used it to put his homemade rabbit hutch there, but the rabbit he kept in it was a pet, strictly not for eating. However, we did eat rabbits, wild ones.
My mother went out with a shooting party and did bag a rabbit and brought it back for the pot. My father contended that the men were more scared by her aim than the rabbits after she shot between the heads of two of his men, making them leap in different directions.

Knitting was a more productive war activity. All of us, boys as well as girls, learned to knit, and the boys took to it with enthusiasm once it was seen to have no stigma in the war situation We spent most evenings knitting squares which were sewn together to make blanket for the troops. They were warm, soft cuddly objects and I could never quite see the macho fraternity cosying into them. Maybe they went for communal shelter use in the big cities, or to hospitals.

We also knitted socks, balaclava helmets and gloves for the troops, all in navy or airforce blue or khaki. For home use we used up left over scraps of wool, and turned out gaudy gloves, often with stripes going round the fingers."

Brenda and Helen earned money for wartime causes.

"Virginia and I used to make up bunches of flowers and sell them to passers by at our gate, we gave the money to Mrs.Churchill`s Aid to Russia. We had a letter of thanks from her signed Clementine Churchill."

"We used to sell flowers & give the money to Mrs. Churchill's "Aid to Russia."

And Helen says; "I took very seriously the raising of money for various wartime causes. At school we were each allocated a Catholic Sailor, to whom we wrote, and for whom we knitted scarves or gloves, and I had letters from him. Then there was Mrs Churchill's Aid to Russia fund. I was recently looking though the effects of a Queens Rd friend, Jane Thompson, who had died, and there was a nice letter from "Clemmie" Churchill, thanking us for the £30 that we had raised by a sale and coffee morning in Jane's house. We had a committee with chairman, secretary, treasurer, including a lovely friend, Ludmilla. She was a white Russian ex-nursing sister, married to a Scottish radiologist, who helped us. This continued until almost all the group were sent off to boarding schools in safer parts of the country."

Another writer recalls her own effort. "A school friend and I made little woolly gollies and sold them for money and sent the money to the Red Cross."

Peter Gillard recalls joint projects to help the war effort, "as well as the legislation which governed many people's lives as to what work they were allowed to do.

Official requisition was one of the many Draconian measures in a time when the powers of the State were overt and unarguable. Women were drafted into all sorts of jobs hitherto the sole reserve of men. This had profound and long term social effects.

There were frequent parades to raise money and aluminium saucepans for `Spitfires` and all the iron fences were removed with gas cutters `for the War Effort` `Drumhead services` were held in Rock Park. At the end coins would be thrown on the drum as a collection again, for the `War Effort.`"

He also describes one of his masters at the Grammar School. "Pete Evans, the Carpentry Master used to sing `Dear Old Pals, Jolly Old Pals` in a loud and quavering tenor at the back of the carpentry classroom, while supposed to be teaching us, but instead, making tiny model Spitfire brooches out of craftily folded, cut and filed pennies. A safety pin would be soldered on the back and the item sold for the local `Spitfire Fund!`"

Children's lives were inevitably affected by all this.

Peter also remembers an unusual event. It was the reward, "made secretly but eventually `leaked` by the lad in question for finding a German radio set in a disused lime kiln on the coast. This was fantastically dramatic. The North Devon coast, once past Ilfracombe, looks directly over the Bristol Channel and across to Wales – of some strategic significance to an enemy." The lad involved had made a real contribution.

There were Government Schemes to encourage children as well as adults to save money eg. Savings Stamps, and National Savings. As Peter says "Saving was seen as patriotic as well as being within the concept of `good stewardship` which was an important element of family life. The latter virtue was really part of the principles of the Open (Plymouth) Brethren, to which religious group many of my family belonged. Adults were encouraged by the government to purchase `War Bonds` and `War Loan` shares. These attracted a low rate of interest, and were `Gilts` of course. It is amazing to see that they are still being traded and owned now, as reported in the City columns of the financial section of the paper. The interest is still low!"

We all gave more than time and money on a daily basis, to help the war effort. Most of the children were too young to have any later regrets about the war stealing their lives from them, unlike the adults who did in fact spend many years of their lives doing things which they had not planned on doing. However Brenda was one youngster who still remembers an opportunity lost because of the war.
"Ralph Richardson offered me a small part in a film but my parents would not let me go to London because of the doodle bugs. I saw the film years later."

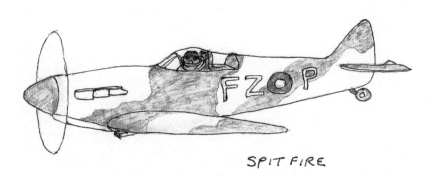

SPIT FIRE

The End of the War

Peter Bruce describes that day which everyone had been waiting for.
"Although the Second World War didn`t end till August 1945, it was V.E. Day 8th May, 1945 when the real celebrations took place in North Staffordshire.

The 8th and 9th May were declared public holidays. Street parties were held, the government had allocated additional rations for Victory parties. Bonfires were lit, pubs had extended opening hours, and there was dancing in the streets. It was the end of an era. Everyone thought that a new world was about to begin."

For myself, the actual end of the war was something of an anti-climax.
The end of the War came when we had just returned from the Easter holidays to boarding school. We had known before we came back that the end was imminent. Mother was preparing to go back home to Essex after our long stay in South Wales. At school we knew which day was to be the official day of the end of the European War. We knew it would be announced at midnight. That night we were in bed at the usual time, about 9 pm. My room mate Marjorie and I were sharing a room. We decided to keep awake to hear the church bells ring out. I couldn't keep her awake, and when they did finally ring out, I turned to see if she was asleep. In fact she was sobbing quietly as she had received the news, just a few days beforehand, that her disabled brother had finally died. I realised that so many people would be weeping that night, having lost loved ones because of the war, but I felt euphoric to have been part of the struggle and that we had "won" the war. Apart from that sorrow for my friend, I enjoyed going home for the official celebration in London. I didn`t actually go to London, as Dad wanted us all to gather at our house in the country in Essex, which we did. He had hoped we should see the celebrations on TV, but our old TV, which he had bought just before the outbreak of war, and which I could remember watching for a few months, wouldn't work for the great day. I was very disappointed, but I remember cheering up when I realised we were going to have a special meal out on the grass at home. It consisted of a roast kid, the offspring of one of our farming

neighbour's flock. I was a bit sad for the nanny goat, but the lashings of lovely kid meat made up for that. Later in the same summer my sister and I did go to join the crowds in London, for VJ day (Victory over the Japanese) This was the real end of the war for those families who had relatives still serving in that far away war in the Far East...like my own. I remember that day too. I was standing with the crowds outside Buckingham Palace. I can't remember the smiling Royal Family on the balcony. But I can still visualize the red geraniums, round the Victoria memorial, and the packed crowds moving as one, cheering, and dancing. It was very exciting, but I felt a little scared. In some ways all the emotion felt a bit too much. The war had seemed over already, and my father's feelings about the dropping of the atomic bombs had been of shock and despair, even though it would mean that my brother could come home. My deeply patriotic feelings were beginning to wane, and our

V. E. Day Street Party.

hope for the future was already beginning to tarnish.

Dot recalls VE day as a day of colour.
"We had a party in the street when the war ended, and the kerbs were painted red, white and blue."

Isabel, always in touch with her emotions, recalls a weird incident on the day. "The VE celebrations were a bizarre anti-climax for me. The weather was cold and grey and so was my mood. For one thing my father would not be coming home until after the capitulation of Japan and who knew when that would be. However my friend Elsa wanted to do something, and I found myself pretending to dance to the tune of someone's gramophone, but thinking all the time of something so odd that I couldn't believe I was thinking it. Elsa was the daughter of a German father, who was interned at the start of the War until his naturalisation papers came through. While dancing I was thinking all the time of Otto's leg, a particular leg, from the mid-thigh down. The obsession with this normally uninteresting object lasted throughout the whole dance.
I heard a few days later that Otto had lost a leg in a minefield in Palestine where he and Harold were in action. A case of `The war is over, long live the war`. The real end of the war came that summer, after the horrific atomic bombing of Hiroshima and Nagasaki. My father came back just before the summer holidays came to an end, and seemed to bring back the sun."

Helen also had a less than celebratory VE day, but VJ day was better.
"In early May 1945 an untimely and serious outbreak of flu occurred in the house, when a large number of girls were laid low. They were being isolated where possible. I remember "helping out" with this situation when on 8th May the great news of V.E. Day was announced on the Radio.
Three months later August 15th took our family full circle back to the Fife coast, close to our last Scottish holiday in 1939, but this time we were all together in a hotel in Lundin links. We went down to the harbour at Lower Largo and watched rockets being fired from a destroyer in the Firth of Forth to celebrate the end of hostilities with Japan."

How did it all end for Peter Gillard? "The VE day was much clouded by the illness of my father. VJ day was affected by his recent tragic death at the end of June that year. We did manage to put up a huge Union Jack, suspended from the gutter and upper windows of part of our home but that was all. As for me the Second World War ended not with a bang, more a with a whimper." How true that must have been for so many.

The Effects of the War on our Writers

For all of our writers, there are still lasting memories of the war.

For some the effects have been profound. Peter Gillard's father died young, partly as the result of the long laborious hours he worked to keep his business running in the absence of his brother, on war service, and also because of the added responsibility of being a Special Constable. Obviously the latter part of Peter's childhood was blighted by this. Terry's whole outlook on life was affected by the bombing and evacuation he experienced. (see later pages.)

Helen's life was changed in many ways by the war "I have always and still do have affection for the Dominican Order (result of boarding school at their convent.).Although minimally talented, music has always been important to me and there was plenty of opportunity for singing in house, church and school. There were piano lessons and a great treat was going to concerts in the Town Hall where famous musicians gave their services cheaply. Solomon, Clifford Curzon and Dame Myra Hess and others all visited and gave their services at a minimal cost. They were boosting the citizens' morale and not only that, music was helping me to fill the empty emotional holes from lack of home life."

Helen learned music well, partly from having been at boarding school.

Many of our writers learned skills as a result of having to `make do` during the war. Marion became her mother's apprentice, learning how to make new clothes out of old, and also from her dad, she learned how to help cut a tree down, and then cut up logs, for their stove, by manning the other end of the saw. Her father also taught her how to maintain a house without the help of skilled tradesmen, as so many men with skills were in the services. So he repaired the leaking roof, and the down pipes, cleaned the drains, installed gas fires, built the hen house, as well as working a full week and doing fire watching. No doubt this all stood Marion in good stead later in life when a house owner herself, if only to monitor what builders she employed were charging! She also learned a political attitude which stayed with her. "I learned how terribly snobby and catty kids can be at a private school despite their small classes, superior education and lady like teachers."

She also learned how disruptive of families the war was. "How the war divided families! No longer could I see my six uncles and one aunt any more on a regular basis, and push the pram around to their house as I had done before. Now my companionship was books; in my attic bedroom (freezing in winter) I got through the Victorian and Edwardian classics from the local library to help me through the loneliness of not having close-living companions as I had had in the Liverpool terrace house. In our new house I was isolated, I had to grow up quickly, I was even the last `man` in the A.R.P. team, to make up the numbers. So Dad taught me how to use a stirrup pump, and other things I have forgotten."

Brenda says that "We were always told that if we were invaded church bells would ring. I have always disliked church bells since then."

It is indeed difficult to evaluate exactly what lasting effects War World 2 had on those of us who lived our formative school years under its shadow. I think one could say that we learned habits of frugality, resilience and independence which stay with us today, and are invaluable to us as elderly people.

For many children, the war was the end for them. Some were lost through the very measures taken to protect them. Very many others lost their lives through bombing. Many had their lives shadowed for many years, by the separation from their parents, or by the loss or separation from relatives and friends and even from the bad treatment from some adults. We, in the main, were the lucky ones.

Summing up

Some or the writers were already thinking for themselves, about moral issues at the beginning of the war. Isabel's attitudes were reinforced by the war.
"We certainly did think about the morals of the state of being at war and were only reluctantly persuaded that it was justified. Once the first shot was fired, though, you felt your attitude to the other side hardening. I like to think that, in the event of another war, I would be a conscientious objector, but the appeal to patriotism is very strong, and most people are not proof against it. I don't think my attitude changed towards it. I was always against it. My resistance deepened and my mind became active enough to marshal further arguments against such an obscenity."

Peter Bruce remembers the war in a different way.
"Despite the shortages and sometimes dangers, the war years were in many ways an interesting and exciting time for a young boy to have lived through."

This positive comment was echoed by Averil.
"We always ate well and enjoyed life to the full but regretted that we couldn't have many clothes as they were rationed as well as food and sweets. My husband to be went abroad for four years and we kept in touch, as he made me promise not to get married until we met again and this is what happened. I had fun and dates, but knew the man I wanted to marry was coming back one day."

Georgina's attitude was balanced and positive.
"My recollections of the war range from air raids and fires, to life by the sea and within reach of mountains. How lucky I was."

I already mentioned Dot's reaction to the wartime experiences.
"When I grew up I made sure my kids were well fed and cared for, and that I always have enough to live on."

Rhona learned a lot from the privations of the war.
"My father would write airmail letters. He met his younger sister in the

Western desert, when she was in the WAAF. When he returned home, a year before the end of the war, we moved to Ely, and that was when I went to boarding school. We never had any lasting school friends, as we were always moving on, and the boarding school friends came from all over the country. We thoroughly enjoyed our life as we knew nothing else. We were happy with what we had, and as a result I have always been thrifty, and tried to be happy with what I have and am grateful for being able to appreciate small things in life."

Watson has given us his perspective on the war, now seen from the view of a mature academic. "The general perception was that we were fighting a just war as honourably as a war could be fought – a view I believe justified by history despite claims that Churchill should have been tried for war crimes over the area bombing of cities such as Dresden in the last months of the war, and continuing criticism of Truman for sanctioning dropping atomic bombs on Hiroshima and Nagasaki. Such criticisms might seem valid in the detached world of subsequent scholarship when the number killed in these acts can be claimed to far outnumber those who might not have survived a longer war. Selfish it may have been, but I can remember only thankfulness that relatives and friends would be returning safely – my uncle still fighting in Europe when the bombs fell on German cities, and my cousin who was on a troopship to the Far East when the atomic bomb on Nagaski brought the war with Japan to an abrupt end. These timescales were even more critical for those hanging on to life in concentration and slave labour camps- I remember the brother of a close friend who returned after three years on the Japanese Death Railway to Burma."

No-one who has not lived through the Second World War can possibly imagine the feeling of relief and joy that it was over at last, which we felt at the end of that six years. But in some ways I am glad that I knew what it was like, both the fear and boredom and anxiety of those years, and the sense of deprivation, and frustration. There was also the excitement and feeling of belonging to the community, all working and living for one thing, a better life, at peace. We all felt very proud of our country too, as we felt we were fighting for freedom for everyone. Maybe naïve, but we certainly felt it. We had purpose, and people of our generation sometimes think those years brought out the best in us all. We were challenged, and rose to the challenge, a matter of which we are still proud.

Two complete stories

It is perhaps invidious to choose any of the writers to tell their stories completely. However, to fit in with the designed parameters of the book, I have had to analyse and make selections as many of the writers had already written their memoirs for their relations, and these have naturally included a mass of personal details. These details don`t necessarily have any obvious relationship with what happened during their wartime schooldays. All the stories are worth reading in full, and I am very honoured that the writers have chosen to share them with me.

So readers are now left with the joy of reading at least some uncut material.

Terry`s Story.

INTRODUCTION.

For many years my family and friends have pestered me to jot down the little stories about my experiences during World War 11 but it was not until a visit to Newcastle-under-Lyme Library that I was finally persuaded to put my fading memory of events onto record.
The story covers the period from September 1939 through to the D-Day celebrations in 1945.
Although the story is in the main anecdotal, I have endeavored to it keep as strictly to the truth as possible, bearing in mind that truth does not necessarily represent the facts. I have avoided as much as possible research and specific

dialogue with my peers relating to the events that took place on the grounds that this could influence my memory.

The truth is an individual`s perception of the facts. This story is a young boy's perception of the facts. To the best of my knowledge I have not indulged in "poetic license" by exaggerating some of the events. On the contrary some of the gory and less palatable episodes I`ve avoided .

The order in which some of the stories have been presented may not be strictly correct, e.g. the bombing of Finsbury underground station and the fire at London Docks.

All the locations are real. Most of the names as far as I can recall are correct but may be wrongly spelt.

These memories are dedicated to:
The Kids - Paula Rainbow; Billy Wand; Ronald Bennett; Nancy & Dorothy Garner; Jenny Walmsley; Brian Hakes; Norman Parker ; Elizabeth Fitzgerald (Lizzal) and ; Brian Harrison; "Quackel"; Rosie; Zoe Saxby; Ron Steel and Naomi Steel.
Mr Spittle . Tom Norris. Mr & Mrs Page. Mrs. Roberts.

It was September 1939. I was 7 going on for 8. Every month, same day, same time, we took the bus from Islington to the West End to see my Uncle "Fred" and my cousin Len. I don't think his real name was Fred but Mum had a thing about the name Fred which annoyed my Uncle somewhat. Cousin Len was a couple of years or so older than I. The highlight of the visit was to "play" but not touch the massive train layout in the loft. Uncle used to connect the wireless to a battery to provide background noise. That was the day war was declared.

Initially, apart from the excitement of gasmasks and the testing of the siren, we kids felt a degree of disappointment. It was not until workmen came with the `Anderson Shelter` that we sensed our lives were about to change.

The Anderson Shelter consisted of a number of curved corrugated panels which, when assembled, resembled a tunnel approximately 7ft high by 12 feet in length and 9 feet wide. These were delivered unassembled to individual households in their thousands. The idea was that a plot should be dug out several feet deep and the shelter erected in the plot and then covered with the soil removed. In practice what happened was that some were erected on level ground and not covered, some were sunk just a foot or two, others were sunk several feet below the surface. It all depended on what brain and manpower was available at the time.

Billy Wand, Rosy and I used to sit on top of the shelter and watch the Hurricanes and Spitfires fighting the enemy planes during the first of the daylight raids. We saw a Spitfire catch fire and the pilot parachute out. As he was descending a German fighter shot him. By this time the German fighter was quite low. One of our fighters dived down on the German with its machine guns firing. The German seemed to lose control and crashed just down the road. Despite the bombs dropping some way away, we ran to the scene. The plane was more or less in one piece but surrounded by an angry crowd of men and women who were dragging the pilot out. Whether he was alive or not I don't know.

It was then that the war started in earnest. I had been out with my mother when the sirens started. We took refuge in the nearest shelter and waited for the `All Clear.`

We arrived home to find that a bomb had landed on the house. There were three families living in the house at the time and we all had to find alternative accommodation. We moved to my Aunties house in Stoke Newington.

Shortly after this I was taken away by some official who tied a label to my lapel and with only my gasmask and a small knapsack, put on a train with hundreds of other kids, destination Oxford. It was the moment of boarding the train the full implications of what was happening sank in, and I cried.

Arriving in Oxfordshire the train began stopping at every station unloading a few kids here and a load of kids there. By this time we were all terrified, screaming and crying. There did not appear to be much sympathy given by the adults accompanying us.

Then it was my turn. We were ordered off the train at Witney and herded onto a lorry. Some kids were put on trailers pulled by tractors. Kids were taken off the transport at intervals, sometimes one, sometimes three or four. No regard was given for brothers and sisters or friends. I was one of the last to be taken off at a small village called Crawley. At no time was I addressed by my name. It was "You come here," or "Get over there." I was taken to a farm labourer`s ( P.C. farm worker`s.) cottage and pushed in, accompanied by the words "Here's your evacuee. He's from London." That was it. The billeting officer turned round and disappeared! The woman I came to know as Mrs. Gough shouted after him words to the effect, "What am I supposed to do with him"?

I was led to an outside barn and told that that was were I was to stay and that I would be called when I was wanted. The Gough's had two boys, one about the same age as me and one a couple of years older. Harry Potter`s cousin had nothing on this pair. They took every opportunity to taunt and physically bully me, seemingly encouraged by their parents.

We were taken to school in Witney twice a week but with the school overflowing with evacuees I don't think we learnt much apart from trying to keep away from the locals. It seemed that most of us felt that not only were we not wanted, we were hated. "Those evacuees from London."

I had been with the Gough's about nine or ten long days. Life was hell. Bullied during the day and cast into the barn sleeping on straw and sacking during the night. It had been a particularly bad day. One of the Gough boys hit me on the head with what looked like a coconut shell . That night after dark I put together the few possessions that I had and ran away. My plan was to aim for Witney and follow the railway line to London! I had stolen some bread from the local baker the previous day so for the time being hunger was not a problem.

I arrived at Witney early dawn. My plan was to follow the line in the opposite direction from which we had arrived and logically that would take me to London. The first part of the plan worked well and I set off in what I thought to be the right direction. I remember passing a field of turnips or swedes and stocking up. Problems arose however with the railway crossing points, which way? Left or right?

The first few days seemed to be going well. Water from streams and stealing food from village shops or scrumping whatever I could find. Sleeping was no problem. There were hayricks and barns which provided me with reasonably comfortable accommodation.

I think that I was on the run for nine or ten days but by now completely lost. Having little sense of distance I had expected to have arrived in London by now. Hunger was taking its toll together with a sense of despair. I remember I spotted a large town to my left and thought I was nearly home. Leaving the railway I spotted a small grocery store with some bread, rhubarb and other tempting goodies. Opening my rucksack I proceeded to take my pick. The next thing I knew was the grocer`s hand on my arm. I expected to be beaten but was taken into the back room, given a hot drink and some bread and then questioned. The kindness was unexpected and I broke down and sobbed out my story.

The police were called and the next thing I knew was being taken back to London. It was some years later I was told by my mother that I had been missing for a few days before the authorities found out. Apparently the police had been informed by the school that I had not answered the register roll call and was missing. The Gough's had said nothing!

During my absence Mum had moved in with Grandma Deighton.
Living with Grandma Deighton was not a particularly happy experience. Grandma was still living in the early Victorian era where children were seen but not heard. I often thought with Grandma it was not to be seen or heard. Fortunately, as my Mum did not get on particularly well with her Mum we moved out to live with friends at Stoke Newington.

School was a little unpredictable due to the bombing and by now the tactics had changed and we were being subjected to both day and night attacks. Hence we found ourselves with plenty of free time to play and to indulge in the hobby of collecting bits of shrapnel, shot down airplanes and ammunition etc. I was still able to maintain contact with my best friends, Billy Wand and Rosie. Billy was deaf and dumb but between us we had developed a sort of sign language that enabled us to communicate without too much difficulty. On one occasion, after a daylight raid, we went out looking for anything interesting. I was with Rosie on one side of the road looking through debris and Billy was scratting about on the other side when suddenly he started waving and gesturing for us to come over. He was holding something in his hand which he kept pointing to. Anxious to discover what he had found we ran over and saw he was holding a leather glove. On closer inspection there was a hand inside! Billy wanted to keep it but we eventually persuaded him to throw it away. In retrospect it was strange that none of us felt any revulsion. We just thought that it was not a practical object to hold on to!

It was just after this that we experienced a particularly bad night of bombing.

I never saw Billy Wand or Rosie again.

It was the same night that we were again "bombed out" and had to look for somewhere else to live.

For a few nights we were housed with several other families at a hostel or school.

A camaraderie developed amongst the families; individuals would go out during the day looking for accommodation. If it was not suitable for them they would pass on the information to others. Due to the increase of the night bombings, we used to take cover in the underground stations. The whole station area was filled with families, many who had lost their homes and most of their possessions. We used to go down early to get a prime site before the sirens sounded the warning. The Tube officials used to try and stop us but there were so many they didn't stand a chance.

Mum used to do most of the searching around. I didn't see much of Dad; he was employed at Mount Pleasant Post Office and when not busy with his normal job, would be on `Fire watching duties.`
I remember one occasion when my Dad took me to the Sunday Market at Pentonville Road. We took the bus from the Angel, Islington. Long before our destination the bus conductor told us that there had been severe bomb damage which was blocking the route and we would all have to get off.

At the bus stop things did not appear to be too bad, but after walking a little way and turning a corner to what had once been a shopping and residential area we were confronted with a mass of rubble. A massive area had been completely devastated by bombing. Crowds of firemen, policemen and others were frantically searching through the rubble looking for survivors. Uncovered bodies of adults, children and domestic animals were randomly laid out on the ground. Nearby was a shattered milkcart and two dead horses. We turned around and Dad took me back to Mum. He then went off presumably to help the rescue workers.

By this time school seemed a thing of the past. Hostel by day while Mum was out looking for accommodation or trying to rescue our possessions, the shelters or underground at night.

Mum came to the hostel all excited. She had found a small top floor flat which consisted of a split room and a small box room. 288, Liverpool Road, Islington, I think. Mum told me some years later that there were between 25 to 35 people living in the house before we arrived. The Anderson Shelter in the small back garden was designed to house 8 persons!

There was an agreement in place that families would take turns to take cover in the shelter. When not in the shelter most found refuge in Finsbury underground station, this being considered the safest because it was the deepest. Nevertheless, sometimes as many as 16 women and children would be housed in the shelter. The adults would sit around the edge and the kids would sleep in the centre. It was not often that men would stay, either because they were in the armed forces or they were on firewatching or warden duties. In practice it worked out roughly one night in the tube and one night in the Anderson.

It was a Tuesday I think. One of the few days Dad was off duty. It was our turn at Finsbury Tube Station. Mum and Dad had some old Polish friends they used to play cards with and because of all the disturbance had lost contact. They had met up again, in the Anderson, and wanting to spend as much time reminiscing as they could, Dad arranged with another family that we stay another night in the Anderson and the other family would go to Finsbury Tube station. They were more than happy to take this option as it was considered that the underground stations were safer than the shelters.

That night the Anderson was full. Double its design capacity. The house took a direct hit. The shelter lifted until we could see the night sky filled with searchlights and anti-aircraft flashes. The shelter fell back killing most who were on the lifted side. Some were decapitated, their heads lost on the other side of the shelter when it fell back. Rubble blocked the way out of the shelter and we were enclosed until the next morning in total darkness listening to the bombs exploding, the cries of the injured and the smell of fresh blood and rubble.

The morning came, Mum and I were taken to Euston Station, to be put onto a train to an unknown destination. It was going to be several months before I saw my Dad again.

We learnt later that it had been a terrible night. Finsbury Station had taken a direct hit resulting in thousands being killed or injured. Our neighbours who had kindly offered to spend the second night at the station had not survived.

There was total confusion at the station. It seemed to me, a mere 8 year old, that you boarded the first carriage that wasn't full to capacity, and hoped for the best.

Mum had somehow obtained some vouchers, I think she queued up twice, which entitled us to a drink and some soup with bread. I had my gasmask and rucksack, Mum had a large case and a small carrier bag. The train carriages were divided into autonomous eight person compartments each with separate doors. There were more than eight adults with children in ours.

As soon as the carriages were full we set off full steam ahead. Destination unknown. Mum said it was a couple of hours travelling but it felt twice as much to me, cooped up in the overcrowded smelly carriage. Many of us had not had a chance to wash or dust down and most of the adults were smoking. It was unfashionable not to smoke in those days.
Ultimately sometime in the late afternoon we arrived at Northampton Station.

Not having had a drink or eaten we expected a soup kitchen or at least water to drink.

The welcoming committee did not look particularly welcoming. Memories of my previous experience as an evacuee came flooding back. At least this time I had my Mum with me. We were made to form a queue near the exit of the station. A very officious official counted down probably fifteen to twenty bodies then using his arm as a barrier commanded them to go outside. There were some who wanted to stay with their friends or others that they had met on the train journey. No chance. You are an evacuee and you will do what I tell you.

Our turn came and we were directed outside to board one of the many army trucks. Seating was limited so one had to make the best of it.

Off we went, following the route of Queen Eleanor, first stop Hardingstone where some were dropped off. Next stop Hackelton and Piddington where the rest were dropped off. But not Us. Three or four miles to an outpost called Horton accompanied by a policeman who boarded at Piddington. At least he was polite but distant. We stopped at a farmhouse in the middle of nowhere. The policeman helped Mum out of the back of the lorry then lifted me out. Taking my hand he led us to the farmhouse. He knocked on the door several times. Getting no response he shouted to the occupier to open the door. The door opened just enough to see a stout woman glaring at us. "I'm not having them here" she shouted pointing to us. "There's enough evacuees here already." Comments were made about dirty Londoners and thieves. She attempted to slam the door on us but was prevented by the policeman`s boot. Putting his weight behind the door, he opened it enough to force us in.

My mother was a somewhat domineering person who also had a bit of a temper. All hell erupted, this did not particularly bode good tidings for us. Probably the shouting had reached the farmer who, when he appeared, seemed to take a more reasonable approach but his wife insisted that she would not have us in the house.

I can't remember their name so will call them Mr. and Mrs. Farmer. Mr. Farmer quietly led us both outside to a small barn. A feeling of deja vu came over me.

There was however a small single bed with covers, and a washbasin. In those days most toilets were outside. An indoor toilet was an extreme luxury, particularly in the rural areas.

My mother was instructed to fetch our food at specific times and eat it in the barn. Mother was expected to help out on the farm and do domestic work as required. I was also expected to help with duties about the farm when I was not at school.

The next day the policeman that had brought us to the farm arrived in a small van to take us to Hackelton. The purpose being to register at the Primary School and to have our identity documentation checked. We were taken to the village hall where there was a pile of clothing and wellingtons laid out. When our documentation was checked we were instructed to sort out a pair of shoes, some clothing and a pair of wellingtons. It was unfortunate that we arrived rather late and all the best garments had been taken. I finished up with wellingtons of different sizes and both left footed. Fortunately, Northampton being a shoe manufacturing town, the quality of the shoes was not too bad despite being rejects.

We were taken back to the farm by the policeman in his little van only to find the whole place locked up and no sign of life anywhere. Even the barn door where we were supposed to live was locked. Without any hesitation the policeman put his shoulder to the door and forced it open. When he left he reassured us that he would be back in the morning to give Mr. and Mrs. Farmer a piece of his mind. It transpired that Mr. Farmer was not aware that his wife had locked us out of the barn. I remember a holy row between the Farmers when the policeman came and checked up on us the next morning.

The policeman turned out to be quite a nice and friendly man and promised to keep an eye on us. Mr. Farmer turned out to have a bark much louder than his bite, especially when out of sight of Mrs. Farmer. He used to let me ride the ponies and take me for rides on the tractor.

There was an R.A.F. airfield close by, Brafield, where pilots were trained on Tiger Moths. In my spare time I used to spend many a happy hour watching the planes doing circuits etc. Some of the airmen got to know me and asked me to do little errands for them like taking letters to their girlfriends in the village. In return they sometimes used to let me sit in the cockpit of a Tiger Moth and pretend to fly.

It was a reasonably happy few months for me apart from school where most of the evacuees were bullied by the local kids and sometimes by some of the staff members. My peers who were living in the village appeared to be faring much worse than me.

Relationships with the Farmers however seemed to be getting from bad to worse with daily arguments. My Mum was at her wit's end when she discovered on the `Grape Vine` that a small cottage had become vacant in a little hamlet called Preston Deanery which was some five or six miles or so away.

So without further ado Mum "borrowed a bike" from the barn and sought out our friendly village policeman.

Within two or three days, thanks to the policeman's help, we were installed in a semi detached cottage miles from anywhere.

Preston Deanery consisted of four semi-detached properties, half a dozen farms and Preston Deanery Hall, once inhabited by monks but now a private residence.

The first semi was occupied by Mr. and Mrs. Haxley, the second by a rather strange but friendly old lady, No 3 housed Mr. and Mrs. Rainbow and their eight year old daughter Paula and No 4 was now ours.

Our possessions by now consisted of two suitcases and a knapsack. Fortunately the previous occupier had left a few small odds and ends together with a small table and a couple of chairs. The neighbours here were far more friendly and sympathetic to our plight and with their help and the help of our friendly policeman we soon acquired the basic necessities e.g. beds and blankets.

Mum got a part time job as a domestic at the Hall which was occupied by the

Harrison family. They had a nine year old son Brian who used to steal cigarettes from his dad who seemed to have an endless supply, and we used to hide under a small bridge by a stream smoking whatever Brian could steal. Mum thought it strange that Mr. Harrison was not in the armed forces. As he had so much wealth and was able to obtain luxuries denied to the majority, Mum was convinced he was a "Spiv".

Paula Rainbow, Brian and I were the only three kids in the area so it was natural that we spent most of our free time together. Paula and I attended the school at Hackelton and Brian went to a private school in Northampton.

School was for the most part a living hell. Most of the evacuees were not able to integrate into the school culture and this was not helped by many of the staff who saw us as thieving dirty, scruffy, urban, uneducated kids who were disrupting the school. The situation was not helped by the Headmaster. To the local boys he was "Mr. Spittle." To the evacuees it was "You call me SIR when I'm talking too you".

The school playgrounds were separated by a four or five foot wall, boys one side and girls the other. During playtime it was a practice amongst the local boys to pull themselves up to look over the wall and shout or throw small objects at the girls. We had been told many times during assembly that this practice must stop or the violators would be severely punished. In practice evacuees, if caught, at the best would have to write one thousand lines after school, or at the worst be given `six of the best` by Sir and his infamous cane! The local lads seemed to get away with a reprimand even if a teacher caught them at it.

Shortly after moving in I was given a bike by a farmer adjacent to the cottage. This inspired my mother to suggest that we should cycle to London to see my Dad whom we had not seen since the bombing.

Dawn was just breaking on the July morning that we set off along the B526 through Newport Pagnell onto the A5130 to Woburn then the A5 for the great Metropolis. The 74 mile journey took forever and the sirens had just started their wailing warning of an impending night raid, when we arrived at my Dad`s lodgings.

The night was spent in a shelter but I cannot recall much of that night, being absolutely shattered by our journey. We spent two or three days in London. Mum and Dad had been going off somewhere leaving me to my own devices in the care of one of Dads friends.

I discovered that what remained of our belongings had been stored at various locations awaiting the time when we could settle down once again in our own home. Mum then decided against all advice that we could take some `bits and pieces` back with us. Little did I know what she meant by bits and pieces! When we rode back to the cottage again, Mother did the whole journey with a small, folding table strapped to her back!

Nancy's Story.

Christmas 1938 began in much the same way as those that I remember during the eight years that I had lived happily with my family, my father, Stanley, my mother Edith, and my younger sister, Ruth. However, these carefree days were numbered, and even I, at only eight years of age, sensed that something terrible was going to happen. Adults were talking quietly about the likelihood of world war, about a monster called Hitler, and recalling memories of the Great War. We were living in a modern suburb of Manchester, and my father was working as a Chartered Surveyor for a private firm in the centre of the City. He was asked to go to Newcastle-on-Tyne to carry out a complete survey of the Tyne docks; consequently in January 1939 we left Manchester, let our house and set out to live in Whitley Bay as long as the job lasted. I went to the local school and very soon acquired a Geordie accent. Very soon it became apparent that the rumours of war, were true. Newcastle was a most important port and ships of war now painted grey, began gathering in the docks and standing off shore. At first it was very exciting, but soon a menacing feel was in the air, and every stranger was a possible German spy. I was a timid child, and felt frightened by the overt preparations for an all out war. To add to my fears, my father`s firm abandoned the survey, and he was ordered home. So, glad to be going home but fearful of an uncertain future, we arrived in Manchester in the afternoon of September 2nd, 1939, blissfully unaware that things would never be the same again.

As we sat round the fire place to listen to Mr. Chamberlain`s speech, my most lasting memory of that moment was that somehow God had not answered the prayers I had said over the last anxious months and I felt momentarily betrayed. However, I`m happy to say that I began to pray for an early victory and a lasting peace. It was not long before we began to feel the real meaning of war. Rolls of sticky tape appeared, and diamond-shaped patterns were put on all the windows to prevent splintering----from what, we wondered. It wasn`t long before we found out! The first time I heard the air-raid siren, I was afraid that it meant that bombing was going to start at once.

It wasn`t until later in the year that this was the case. At the end of our road there was a larger road that led from the air-raid warning centre to the local fire station where the siren was. There was a manhole over which the dispatch rider went to take the message that an raid was imminent, and the cover banged each time that he went over it, giving all the local residents prior warning of the coming enemy. Consequently we were often in the shelters before the official siren sounded. We called him "Dickie Dimbleby" after the well-known broadcaster.

The shelters were called surface shelters as they were completely above ground and were only a brick and a half thick. Not really much protection, especially from a direct hit, but for us children they were total security. There were bunks along the side for the children and some adults, and at exactly six o`clock we took our most precious possessions and went to bed in those bunks. What excitement! We were with our families and our school friends and we were cushioned from the real terrors of what was happening outside. Occasionally there would be a loud crunch and the chatter would stop, momentarily, but more often than not, we did not waken. My father sometimes let me go outside when there was a lull, and I couldn`t sleep, to see the tracer bullets flying across the dark sky, or to see an enemy plane caught in the beam of a search light. One night at the height of the Manchester bombing in 1941, the whole of the city centre was alight, bright enough to be able to read the paper, and the next day, quantities of burnt letters, receipts, letter heads etc. floated on the wind into our garden. Of course, we had to clear it up.

Some days it was not paper that we picked up, but pieces of wicked metal – shrapnel which we collected and took to school to help towards the `Spitfire Fund.` One particularly exciting morning I was going to school across the local park, when I spotted a crowd looking at something, and found to my astonishment that it was the wreckage of a German fighter plane embedded in the ground. I was secretly glad that the young pilot was safe. The loss of human life had soon begun to dawn on us children, when my classmates began to lose their fathers as a result of war either in Europe or the Far East. I remember the grief of the mother of a classmate whose brother had been lost when H.M.S. Hood was torpedoed and the constant worry of the young woman across the road whose husband was fighting in Africa and who listened avidly to Lord Haw Haw, and believed in his lies.

My father was a Shelter Marshall and his job was to make sure that everyone got safely into the shelter. I was very relieved when he came back especially if the bombing had already begun, although he got pneumonia and we all stayed in the house until he was fit to return to his job. At one time when it was impossible to get out before the bombs fell, my parents moved their beds downstairs into the dining room by the adjoining wall with next door. My sister and I slept under the bed. I lay there, often trembling with fear, as I heard the sticks from the incendiary bombs rattling on the roof and praying for it all to go away. That Christmas my mother cooked the Christmas dinner (such as rationing allowed) over the coal fire, since electricity and gas were non-existent, and although it tasted a little smoky, we were only too grateful to have enough coal, since electricity and gas were non-existent. On the following day, Boxing Day, my sister and I were taken to a part of Salford which had been bombed on Christmas day. I have never been able to erase that sight from my memory. It was a land mine that had been dropped and which had wiped out a whole row of houses, leaving only rubble with small pieces of decoration still sticking to the bits that were left. Small children searched the remains trying to find anything of their treasures still left intact.

Apart from them, there was just an eerie silence. Totally unforgettable. The saturation bombing of the city grew less and less and we all settled down to a long drawn out conflict. At the end of 1941 my father joined the Civil Service and we moved to Preston which proved to be a haven of peace and tranquillity after all the destruction I had witnessed in Manchester. My prayers were being slowly answered and my confidence in God, restored.

By Nancy Bostock born 29.9.1930.

Some notes about rationing, by Terry Deighton.

As soon as war broke out supplies of many food and clothing items became difficult to obtain, especially imported goods like bananas, grapes, oranges and New Zealand lamb Soon it became even more difficult to buy essential things like butter, flour, sugar, basic clothing and shoes. Prior to the war some 50 million tons of food were being imported from all over the world. Four weeks after war was declared the first effects of a forthcoming food shortage was rapidly making itself felt. Food imports dropped to under 12 million tons. Anticipating imminent food shortages the Government introduced on the 29th September 1939, a National Registration Day which required every householder to fill in a registration form giving details of everyone living in the house. This information was used for the issue of identity cards, food ration books and clothing books. These books contained coupons to be cut out or marked by shopkeepers whenever food or other items like clothing were purchased. On 8th of January 1940 food rationing came into force. There were different kinds of ration books. The basic one was buff coloured and these were issued to adults and school children. Expectant mothers and mothers of babies had green books containing extra tokens. There were petrol ration books issued only for essential users such as doctors and delivery men. Soon, coupons became another form of currency. Perhaps a week`s supply of butter, which was 4oz, would be exchanged for a ball of wool, or a pair of worn shoes exchanged for a week`s supply of sugar, 12 oz. Bartering became a way of life and swiftly became an industry for those of a less honest nature who used the system for profit. These were known as `Spivs.` Nothing was thrown away or wasted. A worn out overcoat could be remade as a pair of short trousers for a child, socks with holes were darned or unpicked and the wool reused to knit another garment. You would often see children in jumpers of many colours made from the remains of other worn out woollen clothing. Patches were sewn onto elbows to make jackets last longer. Some jealousy arose between urban and rural dwellers. Often the country dwellers would keep their own chickens which provided them with a supply of eggs whereas the town dweller was rationed to two eggs per week. Country dwellers could often manage to get extra supplies of milk, butter and meat whereas again the town dwellers were limited to their ration.